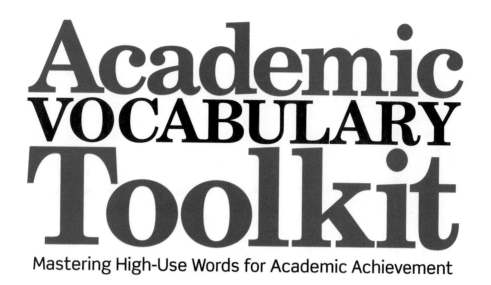

Academic VOCABULARY Toolkit

Mastering High-Use Words for Academic Achievement

Dr. Kate Kinsella

with Theresa Hancock

NATIONAL GEOGRAPHIC LEARNING | CENGAGE Learning

Acknowledgments

Grateful acknowledgment is given to the authors, artists, photographers, museums, publishers, and agents for permission to reprint copyrighted material. Every effort has been made to secure the appropriate permission. If any omissions have been made or if corrections are required, please contact the publisher.

Text Credits:

22 "Sea Jellies" from *Teen Ink;* "Jamming Jellies" by Thierney Thys from *National Geographic Extreme Explorer,* January-February 2011.

Photographic Credits:

Cover ©Victoria Ivanova/500px Prime. **iv** (tl) ©karelnoppe/Shutterstock.com, (cr) ©Monkey Business Images/Shutterstock.com, (cl) ©Monkey Business Images/Shutterstock.com, (br) ©Blend Images/Shutterstock.com.

Acknowledgments and credits continue on page 180.

For product information and technology assistance, contact us at
Customer & Sales Support, 888-915-3276

For permission to use material from this text or product, submit all requests online at **www.cengage.com/permissions**
Further permissions questions can be emailed to
permissionrequest@cengage.com

National Geographic Learning | Cengage Learning
1 Lower Ragsdale Drive
Building 1, Suite 200
Monterey, CA 93940

Cengage Learning is a leading provider of customized learning solutions with office locations around the globe, including Singapore, the United Kingdom, Australia, Mexico, Brazil, and Japan. Locate your local office at **www.cengage.com/global**.

Cengage Learning products are represented in Canada by Nelson Education, Ltd.

Visit National Geographic Learning online at **NGL.Cengage.com**
Visit our corporate website at **www.cengage.com**

Printed in the USA.
RR Donnelley, Menasha, WI, USA

ISBN: 9781305079342

Contents
at a Glance

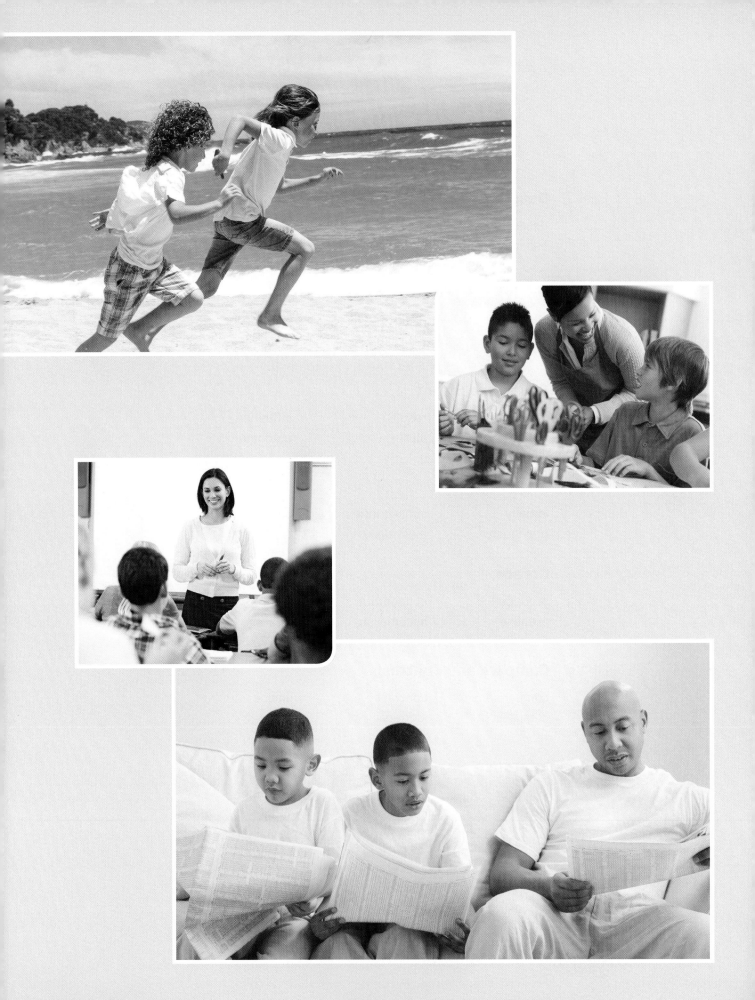

Unit 1
Describe

SMARTSTART

Unit 2
Analyze Informational Text

SMARTSTART

Unit 3
Cause and Effect

SMART START

Unit 4
Sequence

SMART START

Unit 5
Create

⚑ SMART START

Unit 6
Compare and Contrast

⚑ SMART START

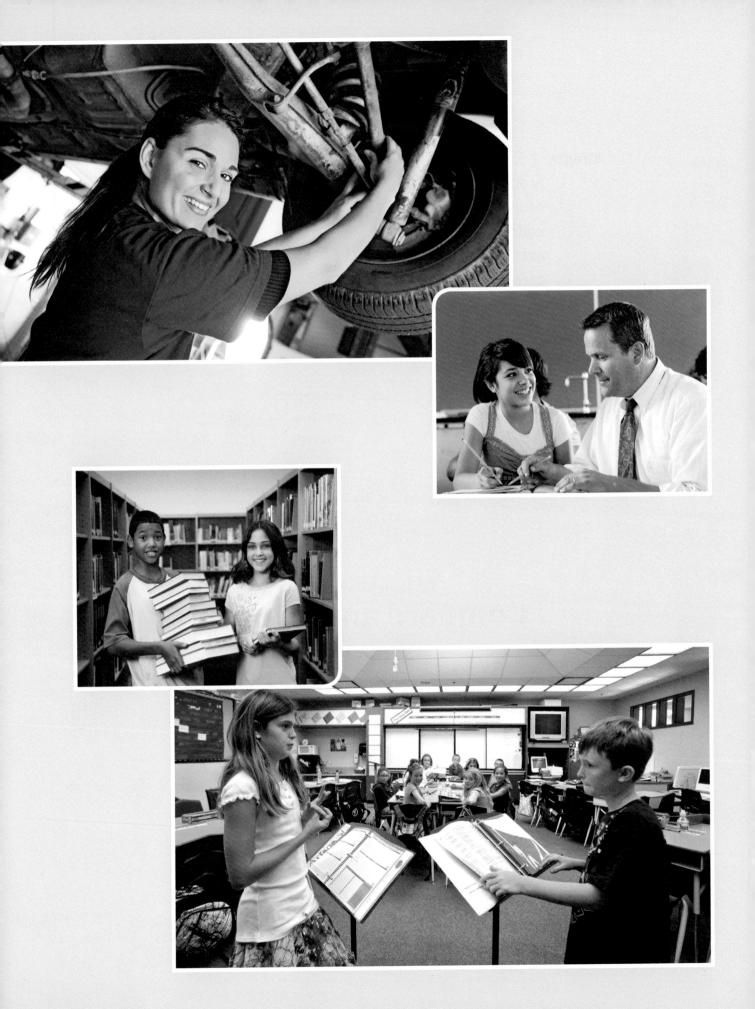

Unit 7
Inference

🏁 SMART START

Unit 8
Argument

🏁 SMART START

Toolkit Unit 1 | Describe

Describe

To **describe** a person, explain how he or she looks, acts, and speaks. If possible, include what others think or say about the person.

To **describe** a location or a thing, use your senses to explain how it looks, feels, smells, sounds, and tastes.

Find It Read the sentences below and underline the words that **describe** a person, location, or thing.

1. Paul is the tallest boy in our class. He has dark, curly hair and wears glasses, which are always slipping down his nose. He's adept at playing video games and basketball. Paul is very sociable and has many friends. Everyone says that Paul has a great personality and is fun to study and play games with.

2. Donner is the best dog. He has a shiny black coat and two brown spots above his eyes. His ears are light brown, and one constantly stands erect while the other flops over. Donner loves running on the beach and is always ready with his ball and leash when I arrive home from school. He is my best friend.

Try It Think about one person you know. Write one important detail in each section of the chart that you would use to **describe** the person.

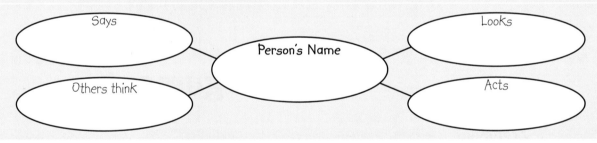

RATE WORD KNOWLEDGE

Circle the number that shows your knowledge of the words you'll use to describe people, places, and things.

3rd Grade	4th Grade	BEFORE	5th Grade	AFTER
		RATE IT		
type	character	1 2 3 4	**description**	1 2 3 4
behavior	trait	1 2 3 4	**aspect**	1 2 3 4
physical	appearance	1 2 3 4	**quality**	1 2 3 4
personality	include	1 2 3 4	**characteristic**	1 2 3 4
contain	experience	1 2 3 4	**illustrate**	1 2 3 4
event	location	1 2 3 4	**respond**	1 2 3 4

DISCUSSION GUIDE
- Form groups of four.
- Assign letters to each person.   (A) (B)
                                        (D) (C)
- Each group member takes a turn leading a discussion.
- Prepare to report about one word.

DISCUSS WORDS

Discuss how well you know the fifth grade words. Then, report to the class how you rated each word.

GROUP LEADER **Ask**

So, _____ what do you know
        (NAME)

about the word _____ ?

GROUP MEMBERS **Discuss**

1 = I **don't recognize** the word _____ .

I need to learn what it means.

2 = I **recognize** the word _____ ,

but I need to learn the meaning.

3 = I'm **familiar** with the word _____ .

I think it means _____ .

4 = I **know** the word _____ .

It's a _____ , and it means _____ .
        (PART OF SPEECH)

Here is my example sentence: _____ .

REPORTER **Report Word Knowledge**

Our group gave the word _____ a rating of _____ because _____ .

SET A GOAL AND REFLECT

First, set a vocabulary goal for this unit by selecting at least three words that you plan to thoroughly learn. At the end of the unit, return to this page and write a reflection about one word you have mastered.

GOAL

During this unit I plan to thoroughly learn the words _____ ,

_____ , and _____ . Increasing my word knowledge will help

me speak and write effectively when I describe a person, location, or _____ .

As a result of this unit, I feel most confident about the word _____ .

This is my model sentence: _____

_____ .

REFLECTION

description

noun

Say it: de • scrip • tion

✏️ **Write it:** _____   **Write it again:** _____

🌐 _____

TOOLKIT

Meaning
a spoken or written statement that explains what someone or something is like

Synonyms
• way; sort; type

Examples
• My friend's **description** of his trip to the _____ made me want to go, too.

• An accurate **description** of a clownfish would include details about its orange and _____ stripes.

Forms
• **Singular:** description
• **Plural:** descriptions

Family
• **Verb:** describe

Word Partners
• a/the detailed description
• the/a/an accurate/vivid description

Examples
• **The detailed description** of the salsa made me want to try it.
• Good stories usually include **a vivid description** of each character.

✏️ **Try It**

An accurate **description** about my appearance would include details about my

_____ .

VERBAL PRACTICE 💬💬

Talk about it

Discuss
Listen
Write

Discuss ideas with your partner, listen to classmates, and then write your favorite idea.

1. The guest speaker's **descriptions** about the fossils he found in Egypt inspired our

class to learn more about the kinds of _____

that lived long ago.

2. We earned an A on our science project because we provided a detailed **description**

about (a/an) _____ _____ habitat.

description
noun

WRITING PRACTICE

Collaborate

Discuss
Agree
Write
Listen

Discuss ideas with your partner and agree on the best words to complete the frame. ▶

As part of our recent social studies project, we included detailed _____

about the many different cultures currently living in _____ .

Our Turn

Discuss
Listen
Write

Read the prompt. Work with the teacher to complete the frames. Write a thoughtful response that includes a relevant example.
PROMPT: What details should a writer include to create a vivid description of the setting of a story?

Writers should include important details to create a vivid _____ of

a story's setting. For example, to describe the old _____ on the

hill, include details, such as its size and its _____ .

Be an Academic Author

Write
Discuss
Listen

Read the prompt and complete the frames. Strengthen your response with a personal experience. ▶
PROMPT: What would you include in a description about the first time you met your best friend?

A _____ about the first time I met my best friend would

include how I noticed that (he/she) _____ had a

_____ . I knew that we'd enjoy

_____ together.

Construct a Response

Write
Discuss
Listen

Read the prompt and construct a thoughtful response. Include a personal experience to strengthen your response. ▶
PROMPT: Think about something that happened yesterday. If you were writing a vivid description in your journal, what details would you include to make it interesting?

_____

_____

_____

_____

---

grammar tip ▶

A **past-tense verb** describes an action that already happened. For verbs that end in **silent e**, drop the final **e** before you add **-ed**.

EXAMPLE: The boy **biked** to the school in half an hour and **completed** his homework before class started.

aspect

noun

Say it: as • pect

✏️ **Write it:** _____   **Write it again:** _____

🌐 _____

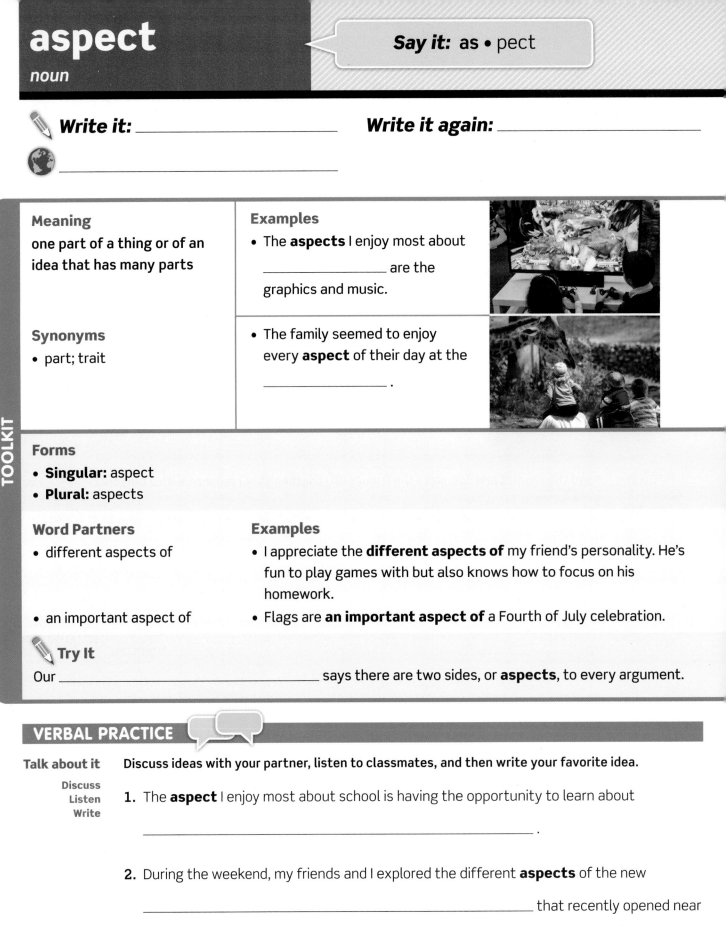

Meaning	Examples
one part of a thing or of an idea that has many parts	• The **aspects** I enjoy most about _____ are the graphics and music.
Synonyms • part; trait	• The family seemed to enjoy every **aspect** of their day at the _____ .

Forms
- **Singular:** aspect
- **Plural:** aspects

Word Partners
- different aspects of

- an important aspect of

Examples
- I appreciate the **different aspects of** my friend's personality. He's fun to play games with but also knows how to focus on his homework.
- Flags are **an important aspect of** a Fourth of July celebration.

✏️ **Try It**

Our _____ says there are two sides, or **aspects**, to every argument.

VERBAL PRACTICE 💬

Talk about it   Discuss ideas with your partner, listen to classmates, and then write your favorite idea.

Discuss
Listen
Write

1. The **aspect** I enjoy most about school is having the opportunity to learn about

_____ .

2. During the weekend, my friends and I explored the different **aspects** of the new

_____ that recently opened near

our neighborhood.

aspect

noun

Collaborate

Discuss
Agree
Write
Listen

Discuss ideas with your partner and agree on the best words to complete the frame. ▶

In Social Studies, we are exploring different _____ of our state's diverse physical geography, including the mountain ranges and _____ .

Our Turn

Discuss
Listen
Write

Read the prompt. Work with the teacher to complete the frames. Write a thoughtful response that includes a relevant example. ▶

PROMPT: **Litter is one aspect of pollution. Explain how you can help solve this problem.**

Litter is one important _____ of pollution that we need to help solve. For example, people sometimes dump _____ on the street.

One way I can help solve this problem is to demonstrate responsible behavior by always

_____ .

Be an Academic Author

Write
Discuss
Listen

Read the prompt and complete the frames. Strengthen your response with a convincing reason. ▶

PROMPT: **What are three important aspects of making cookies? What would happen if you made a mistake with one aspect?**

Three important _____ of making cookies are reading the recipe, mixing the ingredients, and baking them at the right temperature. If an aspect is done incorrectly, the cookies could become too _____ , and the cookies would taste _____ .

Construct a Response

Write
Discuss
Listen

Read the prompt and construct a thoughtful response. Include a relevant example to strengthen your response. ▶

PROMPT: **What are two different aspects that you consider when selecting a movie to watch on TV?**

_____

_____

_____

_____

grammar tip ▶

Count nouns name things that can be counted. Count nouns have two forms, singular and plural. To make most count nouns plural, add **-s**.

EXAMPLE: During rush hour, **cars**, **trucks**, and commuter **trains** stream into the city.

quality

noun

Say it: qual • ity

🖊 ***Write it:*** _____   ***Write it again:*** _____

🌐 _____

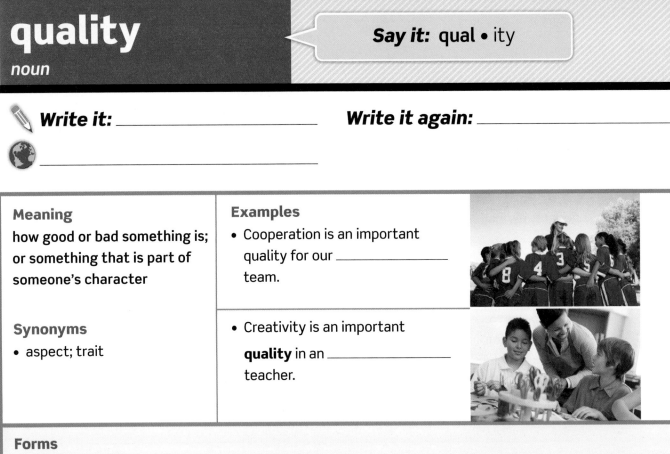

Meaning

how good or bad something is; or something that is part of someone's character

Synonyms

- aspect; trait

Examples

- Cooperation is an important quality for our _____ team.

- Creativity is an important **quality** in an _____ teacher.

Forms

- **Singular:** quality
- **Plural:** qualities

Word Partners

- (have/improve) the quality
- (excellent/positive/ valuable/important) quality

Examples

- Practicing daily **improves the quality** of my piano performances.
- Time management and communication skills are **valuable qualities** to have when applying for an after-school job.

🖊 **Try It**

The veterinarian's advice about feeding my pet twice a day has improved the **quality** of my _____ health.

VERBAL PRACTICE

Talk about it

Discuss
Listen
Write

Discuss ideas with your partner, listen to classmates, and then write your favorite idea.

1. It is important to review your _____ before turning it in because you may find ways to improve the **quality** of your work.

2. Courage and _____ are important **qualities** that all firefighters need to do their job effectively.

WRITING PRACTICE

Collaborate

Discuss
Agree
Write
Listen

Discuss ideas with your partner and agree on the best words to complete the frame. ▶

In addition to understanding people's health and behavior, a skilled doctor typically

has special _____ , such as the ability to _____

_____ .

Our Turn

Discuss
Listen
Write

Read the prompt. Work with the teacher to complete the frames. Write a thoughtful response that includes a convincing reason.

PROMPT: **What are valuable qualities group members should have to successfully complete a task?**

Group members should be _____ and respectful to each

other. These are valuable _____

because they help members accomplish tasks, such as _____

_____ , successfully.

Be an Academic Author

Write
Discuss
Listen

Read the prompt and complete the frames. Strengthen your response with a convincing reason. ▶

PROMPT: **What are two important qualities you believe all teachers should possess?**

Two important _____ all teachers should possess are compassion and a

dedication to _____ .

These are important because every learner deserves _____

_____ .

Construct a Response

Write
Discuss
Listen

Read the prompt and construct a thoughtful response. Include a convincing reason to strengthen your response. ▶

PROMPT: **What is your most important quality and how has it helped you?**

_____

_____

_____

_____

grammar tip ▶

The preposition *to* needs to be followed by a base verb.

EXAMPLE: A baker works hard **to develop** her baking skills. She studies recipes **to learn** about new foods.

characteristic

noun

Say it: char • ac • ter • **is** • tic

Write it: _____ **Write it again:** _____

_____

TOOLKIT

Meaning
a feature of someone or something that is typical and easy to recognize

Synonyms
- quality; trait

Examples
- One **characteristic** that most dogs and cats have in common is _____ .

- My cousin's great sense of humor and his _____ are **characteristics** his friends appreciate.

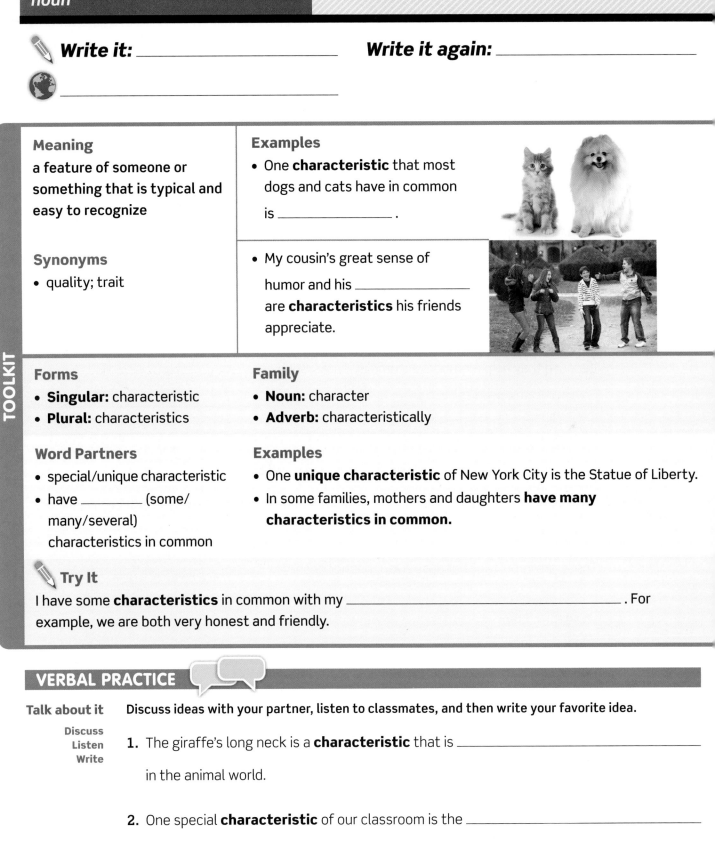

Forms
- **Singular:** characteristic
- **Plural:** characteristics

Family
- **Noun:** character
- **Adverb:** characteristically

Word Partners
- special/unique characteristic
- have _____ (some/many/several) characteristics in common

Examples
- One **unique characteristic** of New York City is the Statue of Liberty.
- In some families, mothers and daughters **have many characteristics in common.**

Try It
I have some **characteristics** in common with my _____ . For example, we are both very honest and friendly.

VERBAL PRACTICE

Talk about it

Discuss
Listen
Write

Discuss ideas with your partner, listen to classmates, and then write your favorite idea.

1. The giraffe's long neck is a **characteristic** that is _____ in the animal world.

2. One special **characteristic** of our classroom is the _____ _____ .

characteristic

noun

WRITING PRACTICE

Collaborate

Discuss
Agree
Write
Listen

Discuss ideas with your partner and agree on the best words to complete the frame. ▶

Many performers who win singing competitions on television usually have

special _____ , such as appealing voices and incredible

_____ .

Our Turn

Discuss
Listen
Write

Read the prompt. Work with the teacher to complete the frames. Write a thoughtful response that includes a personal experience. ▶

PROMPT: What two characteristics do you admire most about your best friend?

The two _____ I admire most about my best friend are (his/her) _____

confidence and _____ . Once, (he/she) _____ helped me

by _____ when I was feeling sad.

Be an Academic Author

Write
Discuss
Listen

Read the prompt and complete the frames. Strengthen your response with relevant examples. ▶

PROMPT: Which celebrity do you admire? Which special characteristics inspire your admiration?

One celebrity that I admire is _____ .

(His/Her) _____ special _____ , such as (his/her) _____ ability to

_____ and (his/her) _____ incredible

_____ , inspire my admiration.

Construct a Response

Write
Discuss
Listen

Read the prompt and construct a thoughtful response. Include a personal experience to strengthen your response. ▶

PROMPT: In your opinion, what are two special characteristics that a great leader should possess? What happens if they do not have these characteristics?

_____

_____

_____

_____

_____

grammar tip ▶

Count nouns name things that can be counted. Count nouns have two forms, singular and plural. To make most count nouns plural, add **-s**.

EXAMPLE: My **aunts** and **uncles** live in different **states** so we visit them during the summer.

illustrate
verb

Say it: il • lus • trate

✏️ **Write it:** _____   **Write it again:** _____

🌐 _____

TOOLKIT

Meaning
to show an example that makes something easy to see and understand

Synonyms
• show

Examples
• The science teacher used a _____ to **illustrate** the process of photosynthesis.

• The photograph perfectly **illustrates** that the boy's _____ were hurt by what his friend said.

Forms
• **Present**:
  I/You/We/They   illustrate
  He/She/It   illustrates
• **Past**:   illustrated

Family
• **Noun:** illustration

Word Partners
• clearly illustrate(s)

• perfectly illustrate(s)

Examples
• The building plans **clearly illustrate** how the house will look when it is finished.
• In many of her songs, Taylor Swift **perfectly illustrates** how it feels to be hurt by someone you used to like.

✏️ **Try It**
• The actor's portrayal perfectly **illustrated** how _____ the bully felt deep inside.

VERBAL PRACTICE 💬

Talk about it   Discuss ideas with your partner, listen to classmates, and then write your favorite idea.

Discuss
Listen
Write

1. One way to **illustrate** how to make a 3-point shot in basketball is by

_____.

2. To support an argument about why schools should have a longer recess, it's helpful to

illustrate your _____

with details and convincing reasons.

illustrate

verb

Collaborate

Discuss
Agree
Write
Listen

Discuss ideas with your partner and agree on the best words to complete the frame. ▶

The television commercial with several healthy teenagers clearly _____

the benefits of _____

during childhood.

Our Turn

Discuss
Listen
Write

Read the prompt. Work with the teacher to complete the frames. Write a thoughtful response that includes a convincing reason. ▶

PROMPT: **The rules of a school illustrate its values. What values do your school rules illustrate?**

At our school, students are not permitted to bring _____

on campus. This rule clearly _____ that our school is focused on

providing a positive learning environment. We value this rule because it helps students focus

on _____ during school.

Be an Academic Author

Write
Discuss
Listen

Read the prompt and complete the frames. Strengthen your response with a personal experience. ▶

PROMPT: **If you were to write lyrics for a song about making the world a better place, how would you perfectly illustrate your message?**

To perfectly _____ how people can make the world a better place, I

would describe how we can _____ each other. I would also explain how

we can turn our cities and towns into _____ places to live.

Construct a Response

Write
Discuss
Listen

Read the prompt and construct a thoughtful response. Include a convincing reason to strengthen your response. ▶

PROMPT: **How could you clearly illustrate your favorite place to relax in a letter to a friend?**

_____

_____

_____

_____

grammar tip ▶

A **present tense verb** describes an action that is happening now, usually, sometimes, or never. If the subject of a sentence is *he, she,* or *it,* add **-s** or **-es** to the end of a verb.

EXAMPLE: My cousin **loves** his bike so much that he **washes** and **polishes** it every week.

respond
verb

Say it: re • spond

✏️ **Write it:** _____ **Write it again:** _____

🌐 _____

TOOLKIT

Meaning
to react to something that has happened

Examples
• Most service dogs **respond** to _____ very quickly.

Synonyms
• react; reply

• After seeing how my aunt **responded** when she saw the price tag on the _____, I knew she wouldn't buy it.

Forms
• **Present:**
  I/You/We/They respond
  He/She/It responds
• **Past:** responded

Family
• **Noun:** response

Word Partners
• respond by

• respond negatively/positively

Examples
• When my sister brought home a terrific report card, my father **responded by** shouting with happiness and giving her a hug.
• People with food allergies may **respond negatively** to flu shots.

✏️ **Try It**
When people hear a song they like on the radio, they usually **respond** by
_____ .

VERBAL PRACTICE

Talk about it

**Discuss
Listen
Write**

Discuss ideas with your partner, listen to classmates, and then write your favorite idea.

1. At the end of the student performance of the play *Romeo and Juliet*, the audience **responded** by clapping, cheering, and

_____ .

2. When the school cafeteria serves _____ , nearly

everyone **responds** positively.

14   Unit 1

respond
verb

WRITING PRACTICE

Collaborate

Discuss
Agree
Write
Listen

Discuss ideas with your partner and agree on the best words to complete the frame. ▶

When a student asks for clarification during a complex math lesson, an effective teacher always

_____ by _____ .

Our Turn

Discuss
Listen
Write

Read the prompt. Work with the teacher to complete the frames. Write a thoughtful response that includes a convincing reason. ▶
PROMPT: **How should you respond when you hear the fire alarm at school?**

When we hear the fire alarm, we should _____ by lining up and leaving

the room quickly, _____ our teachers' directions, and

raising our hand during roll call. It is important to follow this process so that every student is

_____ during an emergency.

Be an Academic Author

Write
Discuss
Listen

Read the prompt and complete the frames. Strengthen your response with a convincing reason. ▶
PROMPT: **How would you respond if a classmate asked to copy your homework?**

If a classmate asked to copy my homework, I would _____ by saying,

"No, you can't copy mine, but I will happily help you _____ yours."

If I respond in a _____ way, it might help my

classmate feel _____ about completing the assignment.

Construct a Response

Write
Discuss
Listen

Read the prompt and construct a thoughtful response. Include a convincing reason to strengthen your response. ▶
PROMPT: **Imagine that your best friend was angry and suddenly said that they didn't want to be friends. How would you respond in order to save your friendship?**

_____

_____

_____

_____

grammar tip ▶

Use a **verb** + **-ing** after the prepositions **by**, **of**, and **for**.

EXAMPLE: By **calling** his name over and over, I was able to convince my rabbit to return to his cage.

description

description   *noun*

DAY 1

The author's detailed _____ of the cold, gloomy

castle helped me understand what life was like during ancient times in

_____ .

description   *noun*

DAY 2

The poster had a vivid _____ of the lost

_____ ,

which made it easy for his owners to find him.

DAY 3

My father gave me a precise _____ of the steps

necessary to use the barbecue to make grilled _____ .

DAY 4

To help us correctly complete our _____ , our

teacher gave us a precise _____ of

what to write on every page.

DAY 5

Reading the newspaper reporter's detailed _____

of our winning game reminded me of every moment of the final

_____ .

TOTAL

SMARTSTART

REVIEW: description

The witness gave such an accurate _____

of the burglars that the police were able to find them in a matter of

_____ .

aspect   *noun*

Two important _____ to consider when

preparing for a test are planning when to study and making sure to review the

_____ .

In my opinion, the best _____ of summer

vacation is being able to _____ .

There are many different _____

to owning a pet. For example, it is very important to make sure your pet gets plenty of

_____ every day.

There are several important _____ to a

good story: the setting, the character, and detailed descriptions about the characters'

_____ .

TOTAL

quality

REVIEW: aspect

DAY 1

One important _____ of a movie or television awards

show is finding out who will win for the category of best _____

_____ .

quality *noun*

DAY 2

One _____ I like best about

my friend is (his/her) _____ willingness to listen to my

_____ .

DAY 3

Two _____ that successful

_____ share are courage and a

strong desire to succeed.

DAY 4

What I admire most in parents is _____ .

This is an important _____ because it

helps their children feel safe and confident.

DAY 5

The _____ I like best about

myself is my courage. I like this quality because it helps me _____

_____ .

TOTAL

18

◣✪ SMART*START*

REVIEW: quality

DAY 1

The _____ of my handwriting is

always better when I _____ .

---

characteristic   *noun*

DAY 2

Two special _____ of my cat are

a big white spot over each _____

and orange and black stripes across her back.

DAY 3

A typical _____ of bullies is that

they have quick tempers. They also seem to enjoy _____

_____ .

DAY 4

To be an effective principal, a person must have several important

_____ , such as compassion and the ability to communicate

to _____ clearly.

DAY 5

Raspberries and blackberries have several _____

in common. For example, they both have textured skin, and birds and

_____ love them.

TOTAL

illustrate

REVIEW: characteristic

DAY 1

Some cartoons have several distinct _____ that convey the artist's

style. For example, a cartoon created by a Disney artist is usually very different from

other cartoons, such as _____ .

---

illustrate *verb*

DAY 2

Last week, we saw an advertisement in a magazine that clearly

_____ the message that the restaurant had the best

_____ in town.

DAY 3

The video clip of the boy playing with his new _____

perfectly _____ how great it feels to

have a pet.

DAY 4

The author's detailed descriptions of the character's nightmares _____

that he was clearly afraid of _____ .

DAY 5

I bought a new notebook for school and _____ it with

drawings of our school mascot and my favorite _____ .

TOTAL

SMARTSTART

REVIEW: illustrate

DAY 1

Magazines such as *National Geographic* include a lot of _____

and diagrams to _____ the adventures described

in the articles.

---

respond *verb*

DAY 2

When friends invite you to go to(a/an) _____

_____ , it is polite to

_____ quickly and let them know if you will or will not attend.

DAY 3

This morning, when my uncle was tired of waiting for the _____

ahead to move when the light turned green, he _____

by honking his horn.

DAY 4

Last week my friend asked me to help her run for class president, so I

_____ by offering to create

_____ to illustrate why she should be elected.

DAY 5

During the thunderstorm last night, my dog _____

by _____ under my bed and covering

his eyes with his paws.

TOTAL

Analyze Informational Text

Analyze means to carefully study.

Informational text can be found in many places, such as articles in a newspaper, magazine, textbook, or even on the Internet. **Informational text** provides important information about something and includes facts.

To **analyze informational text**, be sure to:
- read the title and headings
- read each section, paragraph, or list many times
- carefully study any pictures and charts
- discuss key ideas and important details
- think about what you've learned

🔍 **Find It**   Read the sample texts below. Put a star next to the **informational text**.

Sea Jellies
by Teen Ink

I had been afraid of the sea jellies since I was a child running up and down the beach behind Auntie Sheila's house in Largo, with no shoes on and wild flowers in my hair and smooth sea stones in my pockets. They floated in the rock pools along the shore like milky bubbles of glass, their delicately ruffled tentacles bunched up at their throats like strands of lace, streaming out behind them in the shallow water as they drifted about in search of the sea.

JAMMING JELLIES
by Dr. Tierney Thys

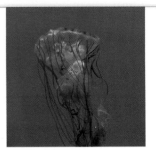

Only about 70 jelly species have stings powerful enough to hurt people. Most jelly stings cause only a little pain. The sting might feel a little like an insect bite. The stings of some jellies, however, are much worse.

In fact, a box jelly is one of the deadliest animals on Earth. Never tangle with one! Tentacles grow from each corner of a box jelly's cube-shape bell. They can grow up to three meters (10 feet) long. Each tentacle has about 5,000 stinging cells. A box jelly's sting is so powerful, it can cause a person to go into shock and drown.

✏️ **Try It**   **Analyze** the **informational text** by reading it several times. Then underline important details, and discuss what you learned using the sentence frames.

One fact I learned from the informational text is that jellies _____ .

Another fact that I learned from the informational text is that _____ .

RATE WORD KNOWLEDGE

Circle the number that shows your knowledge of the words you'll use to analyze text.

3rd Grade	4th Grade	BEFORE	5th Grade	AFTER
important	focus	1 2 3 4	**significant**	1 2 3 4
topic	essential	1 2 3 4	**section**	1 2 3 4
detail	emphasize	1 2 3 4	**discuss**	1 2 3 4
information	precise	1 2 3 4	**context**	1 2 3 4
fact	message	1 2 3 4	**excerpt**	1 2 3 4
example	major	1 2 3 4	**concept**	1 2 3 4

DISCUSSION GUIDE
- Form groups of four.
- Assign letters to each person.
- Each group member takes a turn leading a discussion.
- Prepare to report about one word.

Ⓐ Ⓑ
Ⓓ Ⓒ

DISCUSS WORDS

Discuss how well you know the fifth grade words. Then, report to the class how you rated each word.

GROUP LEADER **Ask**

So, _____ what do you know
        (NAME)

about the word _____ ?

GROUP MEMBERS **Discuss**

1 = I **don't recognize** the word _____ .

I need to learn what it means.

2 = I **recognize** the word _____ ,

but I need to learn the meaning.

3 = I'm **familiar** with the word _____ .

I think it means _____ .

4 = I **know** the word _____ .

It's a _____ , and it means _____ .
        (PART OF SPEECH)

Here is my example sentence: _____ .

REPORTER **Report Word Knowledge**

Our group gave the word _____ a rating of _____ because _____ .

SET A GOAL AND REFLECT

First, set a vocabulary goal for this unit by selecting at least three words that you plan to thoroughly learn.
At the end of the unit, return to this page and write a reflection about one word you have mastered.

GOAL

During this unit I plan to thoroughly learn the words _____ ,

_____ , and _____ . Increasing my word knowledge will help

me speak and write effectively when I analyze informational _____ .

As a result of this unit, I feel most confident about the word _____ .

This is my model sentence: _____

_____ .

REFLECTION

significant
adjective

✏️ **Write it:** _____   **Write it again:** _____

🌐 _____

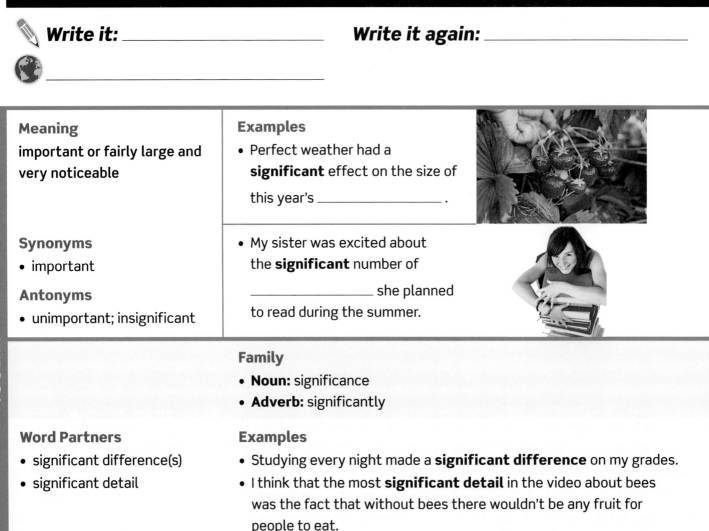

TOOLKIT

Meaning
important or fairly large and very noticeable

Synonyms
• important

Antonyms
• unimportant; insignificant

Examples
• Perfect weather had a **significant** effect on the size of this year's _____ .

• My sister was excited about the **significant** number of _____ she planned to read during the summer.

Family
• **Noun:** significance
• **Adverb:** significantly

Word Partners
• significant difference(s)
• significant detail

Examples
• Studying every night made a **significant difference** on my grades.
• I think that the most **significant detail** in the video about bees was the fact that without bees there wouldn't be any fruit for people to eat.

✏️ **Try It**
One **significant** difference between the brothers is that one is a hockey star while the other is a great _____ .

VERBAL PRACTICE

Talk about it

Discuss
Listen
Write

Discuss ideas with your partner, listen to classmates, and then write your favorite idea.

1. Most students no longer buy snacks after school because of the **significant** price increases at the _____ .

2. Choosing members with the right skills and talents can make a **significant** difference in the quality of our _____ team.

WRITING PRACTICE

Collaborate

Discuss
Agree
Write
Listen

Discuss ideas with your partner and agree on the best words to complete the frame. ▶

Small differences among our race times are _____ because only one

runner from each class can participate in the school-wide _____ .

Our Turn

Discuss
Listen
Write

Read the prompt. Work with the teacher to complete the frames. Write a thoughtful response that includes a relevant example. ▶

PROMPT: What addition can cause a significant improvement in a school's appearance?

One addition that can cause a _____ improvement in a school's

appearance is landscaping. For example, students could plant _____ .

Adding plants would not require a lot of _____ , but they would

brighten the campus.

Be an Academic Author

Write
Discuss
Listen

Read the prompt and complete the frames. Strengthen your response with a personal experience. ▶

PROMPT: Describe significant differences between family photos and those for a class report.

There are _____ differences between family photos and photographs

for a report. Family photos are typically casual and _____ because they

usually capture moments when families are together. However, photographs for a report are

usually more formal and focus on specific _____ to support the topic.

Construct a Response

Write
Discuss
Listen

Read the prompt and construct a thoughtful response. Include a personal experience to strengthen your response. ▶

PROMPT: Most people like to save money when shopping for gifts. How can comparing prices make a significant difference in the amount of money you spend on a gift?

_____

_____

_____

_____

grammar tip ▶

An **adjective** describes, or tells about, a noun. An adjective sometimes appears after verbs such as *is, are, look, feel, smell,* and *taste.*

EXAMPLE: After the first spring rainstorm, the air always feels **fresh** and smells **delicious.**

section

noun

Say it: see • tion

✏️ **Write it:** _____   **Write it again:** _____

🌐 _____

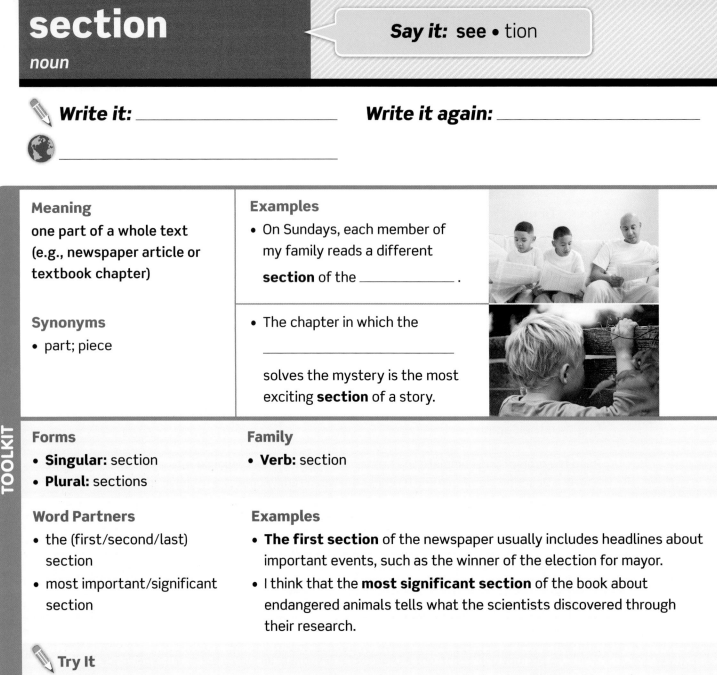

Meaning	Examples
one part of a whole text (e.g., newspaper article or textbook chapter)	• On Sundays, each member of my family reads a different **section** of the _____ .
Synonyms	• The chapter in which the _____ solves the mystery is the most exciting **section** of a story.
• part; piece	

TOOLKIT

Forms
- **Singular:** section
- **Plural:** sections

Family
- **Verb:** section

Word Partners
- the (first/second/last) section
- most important/significant section

Examples
- **The first section** of the newspaper usually includes headlines about important events, such as the winner of the election for mayor.
- I think that the **most significant section** of the book about endangered animals tells what the scientists discovered through their research.

✏️ **Try It**

I enjoyed the newspaper article about Mexico City, especially the **section** about the _____ street food such as churros and tamales.

VERBAL PRACTICE 💬

Talk about it   Discuss ideas with your partner, listen to classmates, and then write your favorite idea.

Discuss
Listen
Write

1. My favorite **section** of the newspaper is the page with the _____ .

2. Sometimes the best part of an online article is reading the response **section** because the comments can be helpful, surprising, or _____ .

section

noun

WRITING PRACTICE

Collaborate

Discuss
Agree
Write
Listen

Discuss ideas with your partner and agree on the best words to complete the frame. ▶

Some adults like to order from the children's _____ of a

menu because the portions are smaller and the food choices like hot dogs and

_____ are more delicious.

Our Turn

Discuss
Listen
Write

Read the prompt. Work with the teacher to complete the frames. Write a thoughtful response that includes a convincing reason. ▶

PROMPT: Why should you read and discuss the first section of each new unit in a science book?

You should read and discuss the first _____ of each chapter in a

science book because it _____ the topic, and lets you explore the

_____ in the upcoming chapter.

Be an Academic Author

Write
Discuss
Listen

Read the prompt and complete the frames. Strengthen your response with a convincing reason. ▶

PROMPT: If your teacher asked you to write an article about your town for new families moving to the area, what is one section you would be sure to include?

If I were to write an article about my town, one _____ I would definitely include

would be about the _____ . The reason this topic seems important is

because new families will want to know where they can _____ .

Construct a Response

Write
Discuss
Listen

Read the prompt and construct a thoughtful response. Include a convincing reason to strengthen your response. ▶

PROMPT: To organize their thoughts, authors often divide nonfiction magazine articles into sections. Why should you preview an article by reading the title of each section?

_____

_____

_____

_____

grammar tip ▶

An **adjective** describes, or tells about, a noun. An adjective sometimes appears after verbs such as *is, are, look, feel, smell,* and *taste.*

EXAMPLE: The cupcakes that my friend brought to school looked **pretty** and tasted **delicious**.

discuss

verb

Say it: dis • cuss

Write it: _____ **Write it again:** _____

_____

TOOLKIT

Meaning

to talk with a person or group in order to share ideas and decide something

Synonyms

• to talk about

Examples

• My friends **discuss** every option on the _____ before deciding what to eat.

• During commercial breaks, my uncle and I like to **discuss** the plays of the _____ game so far.

Forms

• **Present:**

| I/You/We/They | discuss |
| He/She/It | discusses |

• **Past:** discussed

Family

• **Noun:** discussion

Word Partners

• discuss a problem

• discuss a plan

Examples

• Whenever I need to **discuss a problem** at school, I know I can always talk to my best friend.

• It is a good idea to **discuss a plan** for saving money.

Try It

Our _____ teacher takes time at the end of the day to **discuss** a plan for homework.

VERBAL PRACTICE

Talk about it

Discuss
Listen
Write

Discuss ideas with your partner, listen to classmates, and then write your favorite idea.

1. If a friend **discusses** (his/her) _____ problems with you, then you know that your friend _____ you.

2. After I watch a movie with lots of twists and turns, I like to **discuss** the plot with a friend to see if I missed any important _____ .

discuss
verb

Collaborate

Discuss
Agree
Write
Listen

Discuss ideas with your partner and agree on the best words to complete the frame. ▶

To be prepared to _____ the topic of _____

in my science class, it is important to study the chapter and search for examples online.

Our Turn

Discuss
Listen
Write

Read the prompt. Work with the teacher to complete the frames. Write a thoughtful response that includes a convincing reason. ▶
PROMPT: To discuss ideas in a group, it is important to follow certain rules for discussion. What two important rules should the group always agree to follow?

To _____ ideas in a group, everyone should agree to follow two rules: (1) listen

attentively to what others say; (2) wait patiently for your turn to _____ .

These are important rules because they make sure that everyone has a chance to share

_____ with the group.

Be an Academic Author

Write
Discuss
Listen

Read the prompt and complete the frames. Strengthen your response with a relevant example. ▶
PROMPT: Sometimes it is difficult to think of something to say as your group discusses plans for a party. What can help you think of something to say?

As my classmates _____ plans for a party, I can listen attentively and consider

ways to add to someone's idea. For example, if someone suggests serving pizza, I could say,

"Your idea caught my attention, because everyone loves _____ on pizza."

Construct a Response

Write
Discuss
Listen

Read the prompt and construct a thoughtful response. Include a relevant example to strengthen your response. ▶
PROMPT: Why should you discuss some topics with a trusted adult instead of with another student?

_____

_____

_____

_____

grammar tip ▶

The **preposition** *to* needs to be followed by a base verb.

EXAMPLE: It is important **to finish** your homework early so that you can get a good night's sleep.

context
noun

Say it: con • text

✏️ **Write it:** _____   **Write it again:** _____

🌐 _____

Meaning
the words before and after a word or sentence that help make its meaning clear

Examples
- Based on the **context**, I know that "play like a pirate" means use your _____ .

- In this **context**, the word *count* shows that the slogan means your vote is _____ .

WORK LIKE A CAPTAIN ⚓ PLAY LIKE A PIRATE

YOUR **VOTE** COUNTS

Forms
- **Singular:** context
- **Plural:** contexts

Word Partners
- context clue

- analyze the context

Examples
- One kind of **context clue** provides a synonym for a word. For example, "A snide, or mean, comment can hurt a person's feelings."
- To **analyze the context** of a word, you study the rest of the sentence and paragraph in which it appears.

✏️ **Try It**
In the **context** of a recipe for _____ , the term *batter* means "the mixture of ingredients," not "the person who bats a ball."

VERBAL PRACTICE

Talk about it   Discuss ideas with your partner, listen to classmates, and then write your favorite idea.

Discuss
Listen
Write

1. I would have to study the **context** to decide if the word "ring" means "to make a sound" or "a piece of jewelry" such as a _____ ring.

2. When we see a word that doesn't make sense, we can analyze the **context** to _____ what the word means.

WRITING PRACTICE

Collaborate

Discuss
Agree
Write
Listen

Discuss ideas with your partner and agree on the best words to complete the frame. ▷

In the sentence, "Planets move in circles called orbits around the sun," the term *called*

signals that the word *orbits* means *circles*. Writers often provide _____

clues to help you _____ the meaning of a word.

Our Turn

Discuss
Listen
Write

Read the prompt. Work with the teacher to complete the frames. Write a thoughtful response that includes a convincing reason.
PROMPT: **How does the context clarify the meaning of *ecstatic* in the sentence, "Unlike the sadness Tom felt after his friend moved away, he felt ecstatic when his cousin visited."?**

The sentence "Unlike the sadness…, he felt ecstatic" tells us that the word *ecstatic* must

mean that he felt _____ . Using the _____

clue helps us _____ what the word *ecstatic* means.

Be an Academic Author

Write
Discuss
Listen

Read the prompt and complete the frames. Strengthen your response with a relevant example. ▷
PROMPT: **How could you create a context that clarifies the meaning of the word "intricate"?**

To create a _____ that clarifies the meaning for the word "intricate,"

I could think of a sentence that uses the opposite of the word. For example: "In contrast to

simple telephones of the past, today's cell phones are intricate _____ ."

Construct a Response

Write
Discuss
Listen

Read the prompt and construct a thoughtful response. Include a valid reason to strengthen your response. ▷
PROMPT: **Analyze this sentence: "In our business we offer merchandise, or products, that everyone wants or needs." How does the context clue clarify the meaning of *merchandise*?**

_____

_____

_____

_____

grammar tip ▷

A common noun names any person, place, thing, or idea. **Plural nouns** name more than one person, place, thing, or idea. The words *some* and *the* often appear before a plural noun.

EXAMPLE: The **hamburgers**, **salads**, and **drinks** on the picnic **tables** looked delicious.

excerpt

noun

Say it: ex • cerpt

Write it: _____   **Write it again:** _____

_____

TOOLKIT

Meaning a short part taken from an entire piece of writing	**Examples** • The author _____ an **excerpt** from her book that made them laugh.
Synonyms • part; section	• Before we turned in our book reports, our teacher _____ us to set off all **excerpts** with quotation marks.

Forms
- **Singular:** excerpt
- **Plural:** excerpts

Word Partners
- brief excerpt from

- include an excerpt from

Examples
- "Ask not what your country can do for you — ask what you can do for your country. . ." is a **brief excerpt from** a speech by President Kennedy.
- To illustrate the author's sense of humor, you can **include an excerpt from** the novel in your book report.

Try It

A newspaper review of a popular novel usually includes an **excerpt** from an exciting part of the

_____ .

VERBAL PRACTICE

Talk about it

Discuss
Listen
Write

Discuss ideas with your partner, listen to classmates, and then write your favorite idea.

1. The scientist read several **excerpts** from his magazine article about trees to clearly

   illustrate how _____ trees are to our environment.

2. You can see what life on The International Space Station is like by reading **excerpts** of

   online _____ that astronauts write about their experiences.

excerpt

noun

WRITING PRACTICE

Collaborate

Discuss
Agree
Write
Listen

Discuss ideas with your partner and agree on the best words to complete the frame. ▶

Reading an _____ from a poem by Shel Silverstein usually includes a funny or

outrageous event that makes me want to burst out laughing _____ .

Our Turn

Discuss
Listen
Write

Read the prompt. Work with the teacher to complete the frames. Write a thoughtful response that includes a convincing reason.

PROMPT: **What are two important things you should do when you include a brief excerpt from a source in your research paper?**

When you include an _____ from a source in a research paper, you should

always do the following: (1) Place the excerpted text in quotes and (2) Include the source

from which you _____ the text. This makes a clear distinction between

your _____ and those of others.

Be an Academic Author

Write
Discuss
Listen

Read the prompt and complete the frames. Strengthen your response with a convincing reason. ▶

PROMPT: **Biographers write stories about real people. What is one reason a biographer includes excerpts in a biography?**

A clever biographer skillfully includes brief _____ from letters or other

_____ written during the lifetime of the person. These primary

sources portray the character of the person vividly and _____ ,

and help bring the person to life.

Construct a Response

Write
Discuss
Listen

Read the prompt and construct a thoughtful response. Include a convincing reason to strengthen your response. ▶

PROMPT: **Some popular sayings from movies come from the minds of great screenwriters. What excerpt from a movie do you or your friends hear frequently and why?**

_____

_____

_____

_____

grammar tip ▶

An **adverb** describes an action. Adverbs usually end in **-ly** and come after the verb to describe how the action is done.

EXAMPLE: The dancer performed **gracefully** and **energetically** throughout the concert.

concept
noun

Say it: con • cept

Write it: _____   **Write it again:** _____

_____

TOOLKIT

Meaning	Examples
a broad idea or belief about what something is or how something works	• The **concepts** of time and distance are pretty difficult for a _____ to grasp.
Synonyms	• Until 1903, human _____ was just a **concept** in the minds of the Wright brothers.
• thought; idea	

Forms
• **Singular:** concept
• **Plural:** concepts

Word Partners

• a difficult/abstract concept

• understand/grasp the concept of

Examples

• You have an opportunity to express the **abstract concept** of fairness every time you play a sport or a board game.
• To help children **grasp the concept of** money, some people believe that children should receive a weekly allowance .

Try It

People who live in countries where schools do not exist find it _____ to understand the **concept** of being a student.

VERBAL PRACTICE

Talk about it   Discuss ideas with your partner, listen to classmates, and then write your favorite idea.

Discuss
Listen
Write

1. Most schools value the **concept** of responsibility. At some schools every student who

   attends school regularly and does all the _____ receives an award.

2. If all the players on both teams understand the **concept** of respect, playing

   _____ would always be more enjoyable.

concept

noun

WRITING PRACTICE

Collaborate

Discuss
Agree
Write
Listen

Discuss ideas with your partner and agree on the best words to complete the frame. ▶

In order to grasp the _____ of a challenging nonfiction article about

weather, it can be _____ to read the article's headings and review the

photos and captions.

Our Turn

Discuss
Listen
Write

Read the prompt. Work with the teacher to complete the frames. Write a thoughtful response that includes a convincing reason. ▶

PROMPT: How would you explain the concept of the solar system to a first grader to help him or her begin to grasp the concept of space?

To help a first grader understand the _____ of the solar system, I would

explain the sun and the planets that orbit around it, such as _____ .

I would also explain that, if you _____ through space, you might see the

International Space Station, which also orbits around the sun.

Be an Academic Author

Write
Discuss
Listen

Read the prompt and complete the frames. Strengthen your response with a personal experience.

PROMPT: What can you do if you feel overwhelmed by a difficult concept in a science textbook?

If you feel overwhelmed by a difficult _____ in a science textbook, you

can break the lengthy text into small _____ and take brief study notes.

Your notes should give you the important _____ of the text.

Construct a Response

Write
Discuss
Listen

Read the prompt and construct a thoughtful response. Include a convincing reason to strengthen your response.

PROMPT: If your friend has difficulty understanding a math concept, what can you do to help?

_____

_____

_____

_____

grammar tip ▶

Noncount nouns name things that cannot be counted in English. Noncount nouns have the same form for "one" or "more than one." Do not add –s to a noncount noun to make it plural.

EXAMPLE: Lightning and **thunder** are both signs of coming rainstorms.

concept **35**

significant

REVIEW: respond *verb*

DAY 1

If someone asks to borrow a special _____ ,

you could _____

by saying, "This means a lot to me and I'm uncomfortable lending it to others."

---

significant *adjective*

DAY 2

The most _____ detail in the recipe was to bake the

_____ for exactly 20 minutes at 350 degrees.

DAY 3

To play different video games well, you need to understand the _____

differences among them, such as the various _____

you can use as you play.

DAY 4

One _____ difference between a talent show and

a concert is that performers in a talent show compete to win a prize while performers in

a concert perform for the _____ .

DAY 5

The first clue in the mystery novel was _____

because it revealed when and where the detective discovered that the old lady's

_____ were missing.

TOTAL

SMART*START*

REVIEW: significant   *adjective*

DAY 1

Reading about _____ had a

_____ effect on the way I now view

their role in our environment.

☐
☐

---

section   *noun*

DAY 2

The manual for our new computer looks complicated, but it includes one

_____ that clearly explains how to

_____ .

☐
☐

DAY 3

I think graphic novels are _____

because the drawings are attractive and the books are usually divided into several short

_____ .

☐
☐

DAY 4

The first _____ in the *How to Care for a Pet* handbook is

most important because it explains how to choose the right kind of pet for your

_____ .

☐
☐

DAY 5

When my favorite magazine arrives in the mail, the first _____

I read is the one about _____ .

☐
☐

TOTAL

discuss

REVIEW: section *noun*

DAY 1

In my journal, I reserve one _____

for stories about my _____ .

---

discuss *verb*

DAY 2

Last Friday, our softball coach spent 30 minutes _____

our _____ errors with another coach.

DAY 3

After school, I like to _____ all the events of the

day with my _____ .

DAY 4

I like to _____ my ideas with both students and adults

because each group offers different _____ .

DAY 5

When my friend and I _____ plans for the weekend, we usually end

up arguing about whether to go to the park or the _____ .

TOTAL

 **SMART**START

REVIEW: **discuss**   *verb*

DAY 1

Yesterday our team _____ plans to conduct an

experiment to _____ that oil and water don't mix.

☐
☐

---

context   *noun*

DAY 2

In the _____ of an article about

music, the word *pitch* means "to set an instrument to a certain tone" instead of "to

_____ a ball."

☐
☐

DAY 3

The word *save* means "to keep" in the _____ of

sentences about banking, but it means "to bring to safety" in (a/an) _____

_____ about rescuing someone from danger.

☐
☐

DAY 4

The author used the context clue *benevolent or kind* to describe the stranger. This

_____ told me that, at the end of the story, everyone

would _____ the stranger into the community.

☐
☐

DAY 5

Depending on the _____ of the sentence, the word

cookie can mean "a _____" or "a piece of information

sent from the Internet to a personal computer."

☐
☐

TOTAL

excerpt

REVIEW: context   *noun*

DAY 1

Depending on the _____ of the paragraph, the word

worm can mean "a program that damages information stored on a computer" or "a long,

_____ animal with no legs or bones."

excerpt   *noun*

DAY 2

A newspaper reporter often interviews witnesses of an event and includes

a few _____ from their statements in the

_____ .

DAY 3

Nonfiction authors rarely forget to include the sources of the many

_____ they use in their books. But when they do, it

causes them _____ embarrassment.

DAY 4

The _____ "onward and upward" from a

speech by Abraham Lincoln in 1859 reminds me to keep trying even when I am

_____ and want to quit.

DAY 5

Surprisingly, the speech by the candidate for student council included several

_____ from a speech his opponent _____ .

TOTAL

⚑ SMART START

DAY 1

REVIEW: **excerpt** *noun*

One popular _____ from the book *The Book Thief* is

"I most definitely can be cheerful." People like this excerpt because it reminds them to

maintain (a/an) _____ _____ attitude.

□
□

DAY 2

concept *noun*

It is difficult for young students to grasp the important _____

of punctuality, or getting to school _____ , every day.

□
□

DAY 3

At first, the _____ of long division was difficult for

me to understand, but after the teacher explained the process several times, I finally

_____ the idea.

□
□

DAY 4

Science writers use charts and diagrams to explain some complex _____ ,

such as how rain forms in the _____ and then falls to Earth.

□
□

DAY 5

Most adult U.S. citizens understand and value the _____

of the right to vote. They cast their votes every election day

_____ the country.

□
□

TOTAL

Cause and Effect

A **cause** makes something happen.

Ask yourself, "Why did it happen?"

To find the **cause**, look for clue words such as *since*, *because*, and *reason*.

An **effect** is what happens.

Ask yourself, "What happened?"

To find the **effect**, look for clue words such as *so*, *as a result*, and *therefore*.

🔍 **Find It**   Read the sentences. Label the cause and the effect.

I was late for the school bus. ➡️ My mother drove me to school.

Since I was late for the school bus, my mother drove me to school.

_____Cause_____   _____Effect_____

I got an A on the science test. ➡️ I studied hard.

I got an A on the science test **because** I studied hard.

_____   _____

✏️ **Try It**   Complete the sentences. Then label the cause and the effect in each sentence.

I wasn't feeling well, and as result I decided to _____ .

_____   _____

_____ because I packed my bag the night before.

_____   _____

RATE WORD KNOWLEDGE

Circle the number that shows your knowledge of the words you'll use to speak and write about cause and effect.

3rd Grade	4th Grade	BEFORE	5th Grade	AFTER
cause	result	1 2 3 4	**impact**	1 2 3 4
effect	consequence	1 2 3 4	**factor**	1 2 3 4
problem	affect	1 2 3 4	**result**	1 2 3 4
solution	lead	1 2 3 4	**alter**	1 2 3 4
happen	occur	1 2 3 4	**influence**	1 2 3 4
change	reaction	1 2 3 4	**outcome**	1 2 3 4

RATE IT

DISCUSSION GUIDE

- Form groups of four.
- Assign letters to each person. Ⓐ Ⓑ
- Each group member takes a turn   Ⓓ Ⓒ
  leading a discussion.
- Prepare to report about one word.

DISCUSS WORDS

Discuss how well you know the fifth grade words. Then, report to the class how you rated each word.

GROUP LEADER **Ask**

So, _____ what do you know
(NAME)

about the word _____ ?

GROUP MEMBERS **Discuss**

1 = I don't recognize the word _____ .

I need to learn what it means.

2 = I recognize the word _____ ,

but I need to learn the meaning.

3 = I'm familiar with the word _____ .

I think it means _____ .

4 = I know the word _____ .

It's a _____ , and it means _____ .
(PART OF SPEECH)

Here is my example sentence: _____ .

REPORTER **Report Word Knowledge**

Our group gave the word _____ a rating of _____ because _____ .

SET A GOAL AND REFLECT

First, set a vocabulary goal for this unit by selecting at least three words that you plan to thoroughly learn. At the end of the unit, return to this page and write a reflection about one word you have mastered.

GOAL

During this unit I plan to thoroughly learn the words _____ ,

_____ , and _____ . Increasing my word knowledge will

help me speak and write effectively about Cause and _____ .

As a result of this unit, I feel most confident about the word _____ .

This is my model sentence: _____

_____ .

REFLECTION

impact
noun

Say it: im • pact

✏️ **Write it:** _____ **Write it again:** _____

🌐 _____

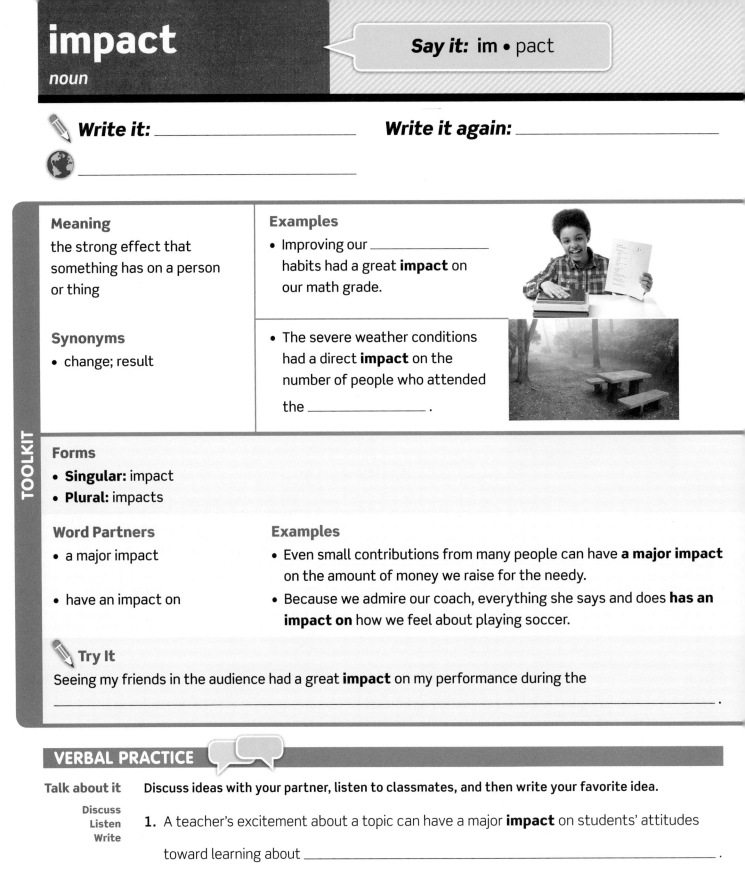

TOOLKIT

Meaning
the strong effect that something has on a person or thing

Synonyms
- change; result

Examples
- Improving our _____ habits had a great **impact** on our math grade.

- The severe weather conditions had a direct **impact** on the number of people who attended the _____ .

Forms
- **Singular:** impact
- **Plural:** impacts

Word Partners
- a major impact

- have an impact on

Examples
- Even small contributions from many people can have **a major impact** on the amount of money we raise for the needy.
- Because we admire our coach, everything she says and does **has an impact on** how we feel about playing soccer.

✏️ **Try It**
Seeing my friends in the audience had a great **impact** on my performance during the
_____ .

VERBAL PRACTICE

Talk about it

Discuss
Listen
Write

Discuss ideas with your partner, listen to classmates, and then write your favorite idea.

1. A teacher's excitement about a topic can have a major **impact** on students' attitudes toward learning about _____ .

2. We strongly believe that _____ can have a positive **impact** on the environment.

WRITING PRACTICE

Collaborate

Discuss
Agree
Write
Listen

Discuss ideas with your partner and agree on the best words to complete the frame. ▶

Many years ago, most people _____ that traveling long distances

was an impossibility. However, today the invention of the _____

has had a major _____ on the way people now view traveling.

Our Turn

Discuss
Listen
Write

Read the prompt. Work with the teacher to complete the frames. Write a thoughtful response that includes a convincing reason.

PROMPT: **What can students do to have a positive impact on a teacher's day?**

One thing students can do to have a major positive _____ on a

teacher's day is to demonstrate when they understand a concept by saying, "Oh! Now, I

_____ !" This will let the teacher know that the lesson was

_____ .

Be an Academic Author

Write
Discuss
Listen

Read the prompt and complete the frames. Strengthen your response with a relevant example. ▶

PROMPT: **What small actions can you do to have a major impact on the lives of your classmates?**

To have a major _____ on my classmates' lives, I can make sure

everyone has a pencil and a _____ at the start of the day.

This will help many students feel confident and ready to _____ .

Construct a Response

Write
Discuss
Listen

Read the prompt and construct a thoughtful response. Include a convincing reason to strengthen your response.

PROMPT: **What invention has had a major impact on your life? Why is it important to your life?**

_____

_____

_____

_____

grammar tip ▶

Quantity adjectives tell "how much" or "how many." Quantity adjectives go before a plural noun. Common quantity adjectives are: *most, many, some, several, both.*

EXAMPLE: *Many* people believe that dogs are friendlier than *most* cats.

factor
noun

Say it: fac • tor

✏️ **Write it:** _____   **Write it again:** _____

🌐 _____

TOOLKIT

Meaning	**Examples**
one of several things that affect or cause a situation	• Serving a beautiful cake is an important **factor** in having a successful _____ .
Synonyms • reason; cause	• Sale prices are a significant **factor** in how people choose which _____ to buy.

Forms
- **Singular:** factor
- **Plural:** factors

Word Partners
- the most important factor

- a/the significant factor(s)

Examples
- **The most important factor** to consider when planning a party is the location.
- Studies have shown that smoking is **a significant factor** in the health of a person's lungs.

✏️ **Try It**

Two important **factors** teachers consider when grading group projects are cooperation and
_____ .

VERBAL PRACTICE

Talk about it   Discuss ideas with your partner, listen to classmates, and then write your favorite idea.

Discuss
Listen
Write

1. The most important **factor** of an exciting video game is its _____

_____ .

2. Washing your hands often and _____

_____ are significant **factors** in staying healthy during

cold and flu season.

factor
noun

WRITING PRACTICE

Collaborate

Discuss
Agree
Write
Listen

Discuss ideas with your partner and agree on the best words to complete the frame. ▶

In our opinion, the most important _____ to always consider when choosing a

mystery to read is how well the author _____ .

Our Turn

Discuss
Listen
Write

Read the prompt. Work with the teacher to complete the frames. Write a thoughtful response that includes a convincing reason. ▶

PROMPT: **What is an important factor that frequently affects the atmosphere of the classroom?**

An important _____ that frequently affects the atmosphere in the classroom is

how often the teacher needs to remind students to _____ .

When students focus, class time is more _____ .

Be an Academic Author

Write
Discuss
Listen

Read the prompt and complete the frames. Strengthen your response with a relevant example.

PROMPT: **What is one important factor in choosing a family activity everyone can enjoy?**

One important _____ in choosing a family activity is finding something everyone

enjoys. For example, one person might like to be outdoors, but others might prefer indoor

activities, such as _____ . One solution

is to _____ the name of an activity from a hat each weekend.

Construct a Response

Write
Discuss
Listen

Read the prompt and construct a thoughtful response. Include a relevant example to strengthen your response.

PROMPT: **Imagine that you have written the script for a scary movie. What are some factors to consider when choosing the music to go with a scary movie scene?**

_____

_____

_____

_____

grammar tip ▶

An **adverb** that tells how many times something happens can go before or after a verb. The adverbs *always, usually, sometimes, often, frequently,* and *never* can go before or after a verb.

EXAMPLE: I **usually** see my cousins once a year, but my grandmother visits us **frequently**.

result
verb

✏️ **Write it:** _____   **Write it again:** _____

🌐 _____

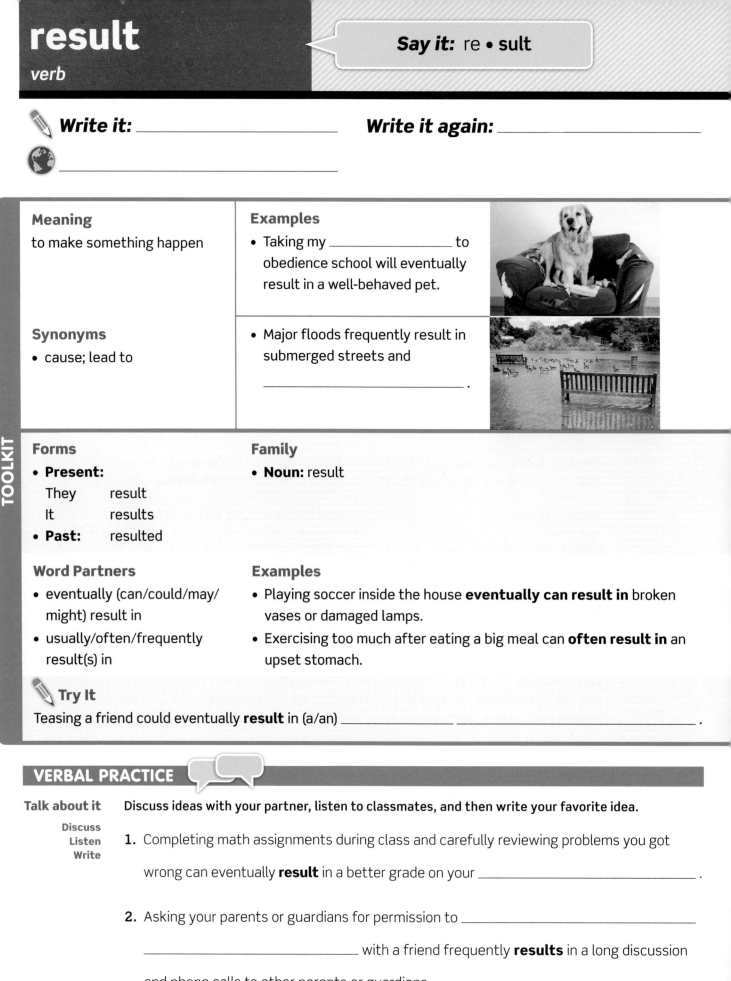

Meaning	Examples
to make something happen	• Taking my _____ to obedience school will eventually result in a well-behaved pet.
Synonyms • cause; lead to	• Major floods frequently result in submerged streets and _____ .

TOOLKIT

Forms
- **Present:**
  - They   result
  - It   results
- **Past:**   resulted

Family
- **Noun:** result

Word Partners
- eventually (can/could/may/ might) result in
- usually/often/frequently result(s) in

Examples
- Playing soccer inside the house **eventually can result in** broken vases or damaged lamps.
- Exercising too much after eating a big meal can **often result in** an upset stomach.

✏️ **Try It**

Teasing a friend could eventually **result** in (a/an) _____ _____ .

VERBAL PRACTICE 💬

Talk about it

Discuss
Listen
Write

Discuss ideas with your partner, listen to classmates, and then write your favorite idea.

1. Completing math assignments during class and carefully reviewing problems you got

   wrong can eventually **result** in a better grade on your _____ .

2. Asking your parents or guardians for permission to _____

   _____ with a friend frequently **results** in a long discussion

   and phone calls to other parents or guardians.

WRITING PRACTICE

Collaborate

Discuss
Agree
Write
Listen

Discuss ideas with your partner and agree on the best words to complete the frame. ▶

Experimenting with ingredients for a birthday cake can sometimes _____

in an original and delicious dessert, such as a cake with a surprise

_____ filling.

Our Turn

Discuss
Listen
Write

Read the prompt. Work with the teacher to complete the frames. Write a thoughtful response that includes a convincing reason. ▶
PROMPT: **What should students do to help create safer hallways?**

Talking and running in school hallways can _____ in _____

collisions. To create safer hallways, students should always look at the people ahead, speak

_____ , and walk at a safe pace.

Be an Academic Author

Write
Discuss
Listen

Read the prompt and complete the frames. Strengthen your response with a relevant example.
PROMPT: **Wearing bulky clothes on cold days can result in your feeling uncomfortable in a warm classroom. How can you dress so you're comfortable in the classroom but warm enough outside?**

Bulky clothes can _____ in my feeling uncomfortable in the classroom, so I

_____ to dress in lightweight layers. This way, I can remove or add a

layer to adjust to the temperature inside or outside on the _____ .

Construct a Response

Write
Discuss
Listen

Read the prompt and construct a thoughtful response. Include a covincing reason to strengthen your response.
PROMPT: **What can you do to make sure that a photograph results in an attractive picture?**

_____

_____

_____

_____

_____

grammar tip ▶

An **adverb** that tells how many times something happens can go before or after a verb. The adverbs *always, usually, sometimes, often, frequently,* and *never* can go before or after a verb.

EXAMPLE: In California, it **never** rains in the summer, but in the winter, it **usually** does.

alter
verb

Say it: al • ter

✏️ **Write it:** _____   **Write it again:** _____

🌐 _____

<table>
<tr><td colspan="2">

Meaning
to change something

</td><td>

Examples
• Wearing a _____
can significantly **alter** your
appearance.

</td></tr>
<tr><td colspan="2">

Synonyms
• change

</td><td>

• Using the coupon with our

_____ dramatically
altered the price of our
Saturday treat.

</td></tr>
</table>

Forms
• **Present:**
   I/You/We/They   alter
   He/She/It   alters
• **Past:**   altered

Family
• **Noun:** alteration

Word Partners
• significantly alter

• dramatically alter

Examples
• Adopting a positive attitude toward the people you meet can
significantly alter how people respond to you.
• You can use graphic editing software to **dramatically alter** a photo
to illustrate your report.

✏️ **Try It**
If you pay close attention to his/her _____ instructions, you can **alter** the
impression you make on your _____ .

VERBAL PRACTICE

Talk about it   Discuss ideas with your partner, listen to classmates, and then write your favorite idea.

Discuss
Listen
Write

1. Planting flowers on the sidewalk and adding (a/an) _____

_____ dramatically **altered** the home's appearance.

2. We can **alter** our _____

behavior by teaching our pet to respond to simple commands.

WRITING PRACTICE

Collaborate

Discuss
Agree
Write
Listen

Discuss ideas with your partner and agree on the best words to complete the frame. ▶

Our P.E. teacher told us that exercising our _____ every day

will _____ our health in many positive ways.

Our Turn

Discuss
Listen
Write

Read the prompt. Work with the teacher to complete the frames. Write a thoughtful response that includes a convincing reason. ▶

PROMPT: In today's newspaper, an advice columnist suggests to a bully that altering her behavior will affect her relationship with classmates. What will the girl have to do to alter her conduct?

To _____ her behavior, the girl will need to be polite and

_____ to classmates. For example, the girl could wait her turn

during class discussions and refrain from _____ others in line.

The change will _____ her relationships.

Be an Academic Author

Write
Discuss
Listen

Read the prompt and complete the frames. Strengthen your response with a relevant example.

PROMPT: How could a major weather event dramatically alter the satellite view of a town?

A _____ can dramatically _____

the satellite view of a town by destroying neighborhoods. For example, streets may close,

and _____ could disappear. The new view would look very

_____ after the event.

Construct a Response

Write
Discuss
Listen

Read the prompt and construct a thoughtful response. Include a relevant example to strengthen your response.

PROMPT: How could you help your friend alter his or her outlook on a new situation, such as moving to a different neighborhood or changing schools?

_____

_____

_____

grammar tip ▶

A **future tense verb** tells what will happen later, or in the future. To write the future tense, add the word *will* before the base verb.

EXAMPLE: Today after school, I **will assist** my mother with dinner by setting the table.

influence

noun

Say it: in • flu • ence

✏️ **Write it:** _____   **Write it again:** _____

🌐 _____

TOOLKIT

Meaning

the effect that a person or thing has on the way someone or something thinks, behaves, or develops

Synonyms

• effect

Examples

• Listening to the talented musician had a major **influence** on my love of _____ music.

• The harvest from my aunt's _____ had a positive **influence** on my desire to eat vegetables.

Forms

• **Singular:** influence
• **Plural:** influences

Family

• **Verb:** influence

Word Partners

• have a major influence on

• a positive/negative influence

Examples

• Spending time with a friend you admire can **have a major influence on** your life choices, such as going to college and choosing a career.
• Playing video games can have **a positive influence** on students' abilities to write action sequences in short stories.

✏️ **Try It**

Watching television shows such as _____

with your parent/guardians and siblings can have a positive **influence** on family life.

VERBAL PRACTICE

Talk about it

Discuss
Listen
Write

Discuss ideas with your partner, listen to classmates, and then write your favorite idea.

1. The weather outside will have a direct **influence** on the type of

_____ we'll choose to wear tomorrow.

2. Reading about people who succeed despite difficult circumstances can have a positive

influence on your _____ for your future.

WRITING PRACTICE

Collaborate

Discuss
Agree
Write
Listen

Discuss ideas with your partner and agree on the best words to complete the frame. ▶

Living in a city where fresh produce is available can have several positive _____

on our life habits. Every day we can walk to the _____ market and

eat fruits or vegetables at every meal.

Our Turn

Discuss
Listen
Write

Read the prompt. Work with the teacher to complete the frames. Write a thoughtful response that includes a convincing reason. ▶

PROMPT: How can seeing the successes of older students influence your personal goals?

Seeing older students succeed at both sports and academics can have a major

_____ on your personal goals. These role models _____

that you can choose your life direction from many different paths. Try not to limit yourself

to one _____ .

Be an Academic Author

Write
Discuss
Listen

Read the prompt and complete the frames. Strengthen your response with a relevant example. ▶

PROMPT: What influence can your text messages and posts on the Internet have on a friend's life?

Your text messages and posts on the Internet can have a negative _____ on a

friend's life. For example, sending or posting _____ messages can damage

a friend's self-esteem. Think _____ before you hit Send or Post.

Construct a Response

Write
Discuss
Listen

Read the prompt and construct a thoughtful response. Include a relevant example to strengthen your response. ▶

PROMPT: What influence can listening to a friend telling jokes have on your day?

_____

_____

_____

_____

grammar tip ▶

Adjectives are always singular even if they describe a plural noun. Do not add **-s** to adjectives that describe plural nouns.

EXAMPLE: *Ripped* jeans and *big* earrings were popular in the 1980s.

outcome

noun

Say it: out • come

✏️ **Write it:** _____ **Write it again:** _____

🌐 _____

TOOLKIT

Meaning

the final result of a meeting, activity, or process, especially when people are unsure what will happen

Synonyms

• result

Examples

• My sister's 3-point shot influenced the **outcome** of the _____ game.

• The **outcome** of the pet show was surprising. No one predicted that the _____ would win.

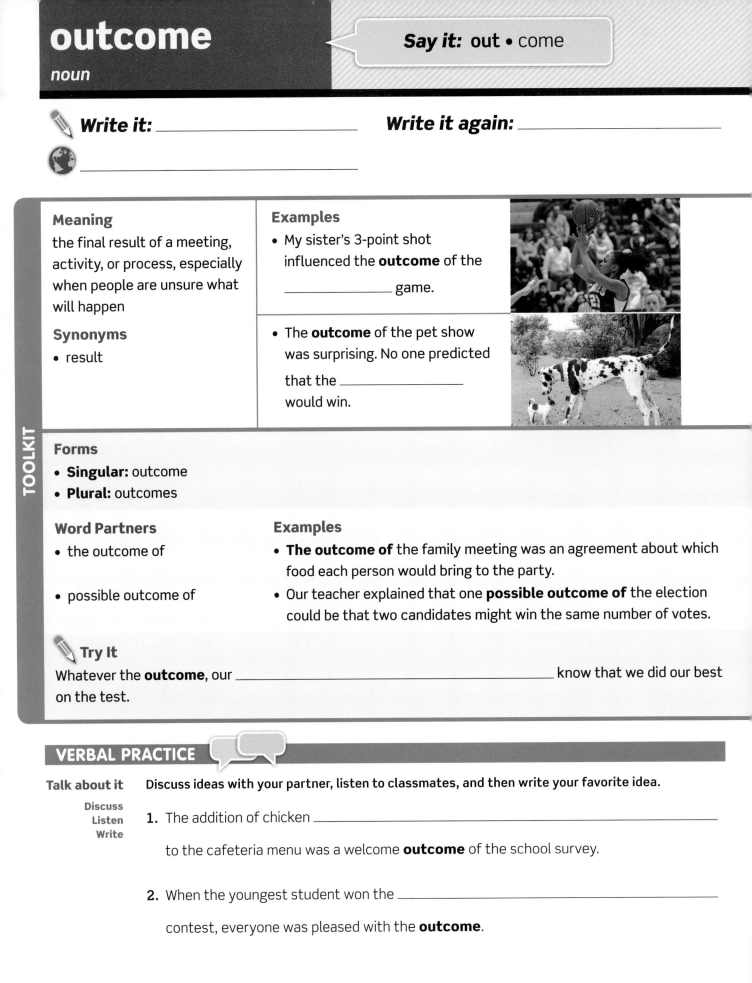

Forms

• **Singular:** outcome
• **Plural:** outcomes

Word Partners

• the outcome of

• possible outcome of

Examples

• **The outcome of** the family meeting was an agreement about which food each person would bring to the party.

• Our teacher explained that one **possible outcome of** the election could be that two candidates might win the same number of votes.

✏️ **Try It**

Whatever the **outcome**, our _____ know that we did our best on the test.

VERBAL PRACTICE

Talk about it   Discuss ideas with your partner, listen to classmates, and then write your favorite idea.

Discuss
Listen
Write

1. The addition of chicken _____ to the cafeteria menu was a welcome **outcome** of the school survey.

2. When the youngest student won the _____ contest, everyone was pleased with the **outcome**.

outcome
noun

WRITING PRACTICE

Collaborate

Discuss
Agree
Write
Listen

Discuss ideas with your partner and agree on the best words to complete the frame. ▶

The band was upset by the sloppy _____ of the performance at the game. How unfortunate that a dog ran onto the field, causing the musicians to _____ in different directions.

Our Turn

Discuss
Listen
Write

Read the prompt. Work with the teacher to complete the frames. Write a thoughtful response that includes a convincing reason. ▶
PROMPT: How should you respond if the outcome of a competition does not go your way?

If a competition results in an unhappy _____ , try not to feel envious or angry. Smile _____ and congratulate the winning team. Then _____ to win the next competition.

Be an Academic Author

Write
Discuss
Listen

Read the prompt and complete the frames. Strengthen your response with a relevant example. ▶
PROMPT: If you were asked to write an article to predict the outcome of a school-wide spelling bee, what traits would you expect to find in the winner?

The winner of a spelling bee is typically a student who _____ the Greek and Latin roots of many words. I predict that the _____ of the school-wide spelling bee will be that a 5th grader who gets straight A's on spelling tests and loves to use _____ words will win.

Construct a Response

Write
Discuss
Listen

Read the prompt and construct a thoughtful response. Include a convincing reason to strengthen your response. ▶
PROMPT: What could be one possible negative outcome of leaving your pet alone at home all day, and what can you do to prevent the negative outcome?

_____

_____

_____

_____

grammar tip ▶

An **adjective** describes, or tells about, a noun. An **adjective** sometimes appears after verbs such as *is, are, look, feel, smell,* and *taste.*

EXAMPLE: After the rain, the air always smells **fresh** and plants always look **healthy** and **bright**.

impact

 SMARTSTART

REVIEW: **concept** *noun*

DAY 1

Knowing when to ask a question in class is a difficult _____

for some students because it is hard to tell when the teacher is ready to

_____ and answer questions.

---

impact *noun*

DAY 2

My grandmother had a major _____ on my ability to prepare

delicious food. She made the best _____ in the world, and

watching her taught me how to make it, too.

DAY 3

Your attitude about school can have a major _____ on your

friend's behavior. If you _____ ,

your friend might, too.

DAY 4

The weather can have an _____ on our family holiday

choices. If it is hot and sunny, we usually go to a beach; if it is cold we usually go to (a/an)

_____ _____ .

DAY 5

The trip to the New York Metropolitan Museum of Art had a major

_____ on my neighbor's life. Not only did he major in art, but he also

_____ .

TOTAL

SMART START

REVIEW: impact *noun*

DAY 1

The weather always has a major _____

on what _____ ☐

I choose to wear to school. ☐

factor *noun*

DAY 2

The amount of sleep I get at night is always a significant _____ ☐

on whether or not I get a good grade on a _____ . ☐

DAY 3

The pictures and _____ that accompany an article about

historical events are important _____ in my ☐

understanding of the period. ☐

DAY 4

The extra practice sessions coach required last week were major

_____ in our winning the ☐

game on _____ . ☐

DAY 5

Making no mistakes is the most important _____ ☐

in a successful performance on a televised talent _____ . ☐

TOTAL

result

SMARTSTART

REVIEW: factor *noun*

DAY 1

Measuring ingredients carefully is a crucial _____ ☐

in producing tasty cakes and _____ . ☐

---

result *verb*

DAY 2

Adding too much salt to the fried rice _____

in a _____ ☐

meal yesterday. ☐

DAY 3

In the movie we saw yesterday, the wild spaceship chase

_____ in the hero reaching the ☐

home planet _____ . ☐

DAY 4

Frequent after-school practice and lots of coaching can

_____ in superior ☐

_____ performances by our team. ☐

DAY 5

Regularly forgetting to _____ the garden

will eventually _____ ☐

in weak, ailing plants. ☐

TOTAL

alter

SMART START

REVIEW: result *verb*

DAY 1

Bad eating habits eventually can ______________________ in poor ☐
health, such as soft bones and ______________________ . ☐

alter *verb*

DAY 2

Good eating habits can significantly ______________________
your overall well-being by building up strong ______________________ ☐
and improving your appearance. ☐

DAY 3

If I can ______________________ the angle from which I view a
painting, I will probably ______________________ things about the ☐
painting I hadn't before. ☐

DAY 4

A clever author often adds a twist to the plot that completely
______________________ your perception of a major character and ☐
the reasons for his ______________________ . ☐

DAY 5

Major earthquake damage on the ______________________ forced
the bus driver to ______________________ ☐
her route into the city. ☐

TOTAL

influence

DAY 1

REVIEW: alter *verb*

To _____ my mood for the day, all I have to do

is listen to my _____ tell jokes.

influence *noun*

DAY 2

Looking at the photographs in the *National Geographic Magazine* had a major

_____ on my choice to seriously consider

a _____ in photography.

DAY 3

Watching an educational _____ on television can strengthen

children's language skills and have a powerful _____ on their

English vocabulary.

DAY 4

Wearing loose, comfortable clothes can have a critical _____

on my ability to run and _____ during P.E. class.

DAY 5

It has been my experience that your culture can have a major

_____ on the types of _____

you enjoy.

TOTAL

SMARTSTART

REVIEW: influence *noun*

DAY 1

The report about the damage from the hurricane in the Bahamas had a negative

_____ on my dreams of _____ □

there. □

---

outcome *noun*

DAY 2

One confusing _____ of the family meeting left us all feeling

a bit uncertain about our plans for the _____ on Saturday □

because we never decided where the event would take place. □

DAY 3

Because the _____ practiced hard all week, the

many positive _____ of the concert pleased □

everyone. □

DAY 4

The last scene of the movie showed an _____ we had not

imagined. Everyone thought that the princess would agree to marry the prince, but instead □

she rebelled and chose the humble and _____ son of the baker. □

DAY 5

Because we compared prices at various stores, my _____

and I achieved the only _____ of our shopping trip we hoped □

for because we stayed within our budget. □

TOTAL

Toolkit Unit 4 | Sequence

Sequence

Sequence is the order in which events happen.

Use the signal words such as *first*, *next* and *last*, along with the Toolkit words in this unit to help you analyze, discuss, and write about the **sequence** of events.

Find It Read the sentences. Determine the sequence and write **1st**, **2nd**, and **3rd** to show the order in which the events happen.

1. _____ That night, we found Fluffy asleep in a corner of my bedroom closet.

   _____ So we looked for her all over the neighborhood, calling her name. But Fluffy did not respond.

   _____ One evening last summer, we couldn't find our cat, Fluffy.

2. _____ The next day, our teacher gave each group its assignment and tasks.

   _____ Then we voted to decide on the topic for our class project.

   _____ Before the class project, our class discussed and listed possible topics on the board.

Try It Show the **sequence** by describing something that might occur after the first and second events.

1. On Saturday morning, my family decided to have breakfast at a restaurant.

2. At the restaurant, we noticed that the menu had both breakfast and lunch items, such as

   _____ .

3. It was hard to decide, but in the end I ordered (a/the) _____ _____

   from the (breakfast/lunch) _____ side of the menu.

RATE WORD KNOWLEDGE

Circle the number that shows your knowledge of the words you'll use to speak and write about sequence.

3rd Grade	4th Grade	BEFORE	5th Grade	AFTER
order	process	1 2 3 4	**initially**	1 2 3 4
next	final	1 2 3 4	**previously**	1 2 3 4
before	afterward	1 2 3 4	**subsequently**	1 2 3 4
after	following	1 2 3 4	**eventually**	1 2 3 4
finally	previous	1 2 3 4	**ultimately**	1 2 3 4
following	prior	1 2 3 4	**preceding**	1 2 3 4

DISCUSSION GUIDE
- Form groups of four.
- Assign letters to each person.
- Each group member takes a turn leading a discussion.
- Prepare to report about one word.

Ⓐ Ⓑ
Ⓓ Ⓒ

DISCUSS WORDS

Discuss how well you know the fifth grade words. Then, report to the class how you rated each word.

GROUP LEADER **Ask**

So, _____ what do you know
(NAME)

about the word _____ ?

GROUP MEMBERS **Discuss**

1 = I **don't recognize** the word _____ .

I need to learn what it means.

2 = I **recognize** the word _____ ,

but I need to learn the meaning.

3 = I'm **familiar** with the word _____ .

I think it means _____ .

4 = I **know** the word _____ .

It's a _____ , and it means _____ .
(PART OF SPEECH)

Here is my example sentence: _____ .

REPORTER **Report Word Knowledge**

Our group gave the word _____ a rating of _____ because _____ .

SET A GOAL AND REFLECT

First, set a vocabulary goal for this unit by selecting at least three words that you plan to thoroughly learn. At the end of the unit, return to this page and write a reflection about one word you have mastered.

GOAL

During this unit I plan to thoroughly learn the words _____ ,

_____ , and _____ . Increasing my word knowledge will

help me speak and write effectively about _____ .

As a result of this unit, I feel most confident about the word _____ .

This is my model sentence: _____

_____ .

REFLECTION

initially
adverb

Write it: _____ **Write it again:** _____

_____

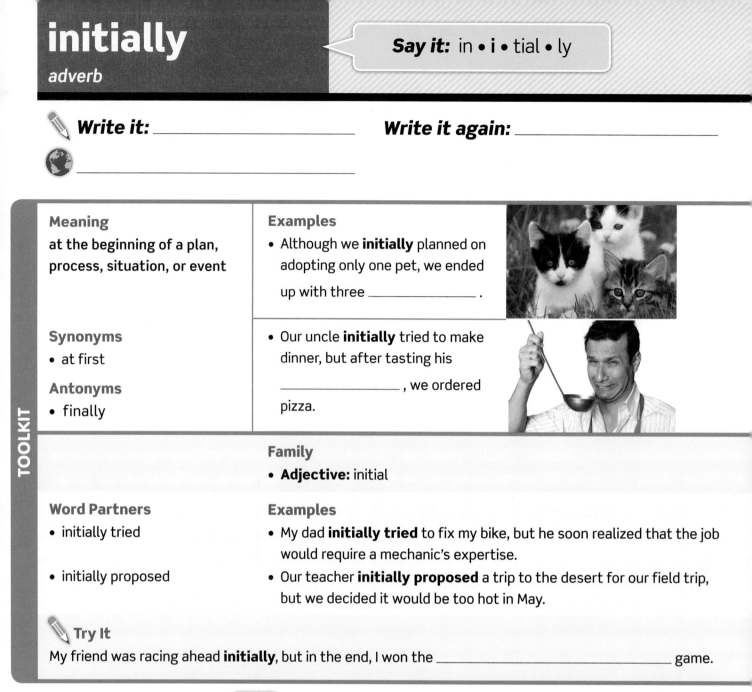

TOOLKIT

Meaning
at the beginning of a plan, process, situation, or event

Synonyms
• at first

Antonyms
• finally

Examples
• Although we **initially** planned on adopting only one pet, we ended up with three _____ .

• Our uncle **initially** tried to make dinner, but after tasting his _____ , we ordered pizza.

Family
• **Adjective:** initial

Word Partners
• initially tried

• initially proposed

Examples
• My dad **initially tried** to fix my bike, but he soon realized that the job would require a mechanic's expertise.
• Our teacher **initially proposed** a trip to the desert for our field trip, but we decided it would be too hot in May.

Try It

My friend was racing ahead **initially**, but in the end, I won the _____ game.

VERBAL PRACTICE

Talk about it   Discuss ideas with your partner, listen to classmates, and then write your favorite idea.

Discuss
Listen
Write

1. To get a good picture of the Grand Canyon, I **initially** tried using my cell phone. However, I found that my digital camera got a better _____ .

2. My family and I **initially** proposed watching an action-adventure movie and then having _____ for dinner. However, after seeing the long line at the theater, we went to the restaurant first.

WRITING PRACTICE

Collaborate

Discuss
Agree
Write
Listen

Discuss ideas with your partner and agree on the best words to complete the frame. ▷

Young children _____ think birthday gifts magically appear. However, as they

mature, children begin to _____ that presents are purchased

or made by family and friends.

Our Turn

Discuss
Listen
Write

Read the prompt. Work with the teacher to complete the frames. Write a thoughtful response that includes a relevant example. ▷

PROMPT: **Initially learning to ride a skateboard can be difficult. What would you do to encourage a friend to keep trying?**

If a friend _____ struggles when learning to ride a skateboard, I would

encourage (him/her) _____ not to give up. I would also try to _____

how to do a few _____ , and how to balance on bumpy roads.

Be an Academic Author

Write
Discuss
Listen

Read the prompt and complete the frames. Strengthen your response with a relevant example. ▷

PROMPT: **How can someone influence what you initially think about a new food?**

Someone else's _____ might change what I _____

think about a new food. For example, when my friend said that she loved eating

_____ food, I decided to give _____ another try

and actually enjoyed it.

Construct a Response

Write
Discuss
Listen

Read the prompt and construct a thoughtful response. Include a relevant example to strengthen your response. ▷

PROMPT: **Sometimes a pet's appearance can affect a child's first impression and level of comfort. Describe how a positive or negative experience with a pet changed how you initially reacted.**

_____

_____

_____

grammar tip ▷

An **adverb** describes an action. Adverbs usually end in **-ly** and come after the verb to describe how the action is done.

EXAMPLE: The student **carelessly** sent a text to the wrong friend and **accidentally** spoiled the surprise.

previously
adverb

Say it: pre • vi • ous • ly

✏️ **Write it:** _____   **Write it again:** _____

🌐 _____

TOOLKIT

Meaning	**Examples**
before now, or before a certain time	• Before he came to our school, our teacher had previously _____ in Mexico.
Synonyms • earlier; beforehand **Antonyms** • after; later	• **Previously,** my friend seemed bored at the amusement park, but he became excited after riding the _____ .

Family
• **Adjective:** previous

Word Partners
• had previously been

• Previously, _____

Examples
• The community library that **had previously been** small was remodeled into an elegant, large space for readers of all ages.
• **Previously,** we studied plant growth in science class, but now we are learning about rocks and soil.

✏️ **Try It**

As a fifth grader, movies that **previously** seemed terrifying now seem _____ .

VERBAL PRACTICE 💬

Talk about it

Discuss
Listen
Write

Discuss ideas with your partner, listen to classmates, and then write your favorite idea.

1. Hairstyles that had **previously** been very stylish and sophisticated can look

_____ today.

2. **Previously,** our family had only planted onions in our garden, but this summer

we've decided to plant our favorite vegetables such as green beans, lettuce, and

_____ .

WRITING PRACTICE

Collaborate

Discuss
Agree
Write
Listen

Discuss ideas with your partner and agree on the best words to complete the frame. ▶

The doctor's treatment of the patient's injured back had _____ been helpful, but

further treatments will be _____ to make him even more comfortable.

Our Turn

Discuss
Listen
Write

Read the prompt. Work with the teacher to complete the frames. Write a thoughtful response that includes a convincing reason.
PROMPT: How can ideas that had previously been thought impossible inspire you today?

_____ , when our grandparents were children, they could not imagine a phone

that was not connected to a wall. In recent years, scientists _____

the cell phone using wireless technology. This proves that humans can accomplish

_____ tasks earlier generations thought impossible.

Be an Academic Author

Write
Discuss
Listen

Read the prompt and complete the frames. Strengthen your response with a personal experience.
PROMPT: Describe an activity you now actually enjoy that you previously did not.

_____ , when I was five, I did not enjoy

going to the mall. Now that I'm older and can go shopping with friends to purchase

_____ , I actually enjoy spending time at the

mall, especially the store _____ .

Construct a Response

Write
Discuss
Listen

Read the prompt and construct a thoughtful response. Include a personal experience to strengthen your response.
PROMPT: Describe a book that previously seemed interesting but now seems childish.

_____

_____

_____

_____

grammar tip ▶

A **possessive noun** shows ownership. Possessive nouns always have apostrophes. For one owner, add **'s** to a singular noun. For more than one owner, add **s'** to the plural noun.

EXAMPLE: The **teacher's** handwriting is perfect but the **students'** notes are unreadable!

subsequently
adverb

sub • se • quent • ly

Say it: sub • se • quent • ly

Write it: _____ **Write it again:** _____

_____

TOOLKIT

Meaning
after an event or situation in the past

Examples
- When the sun rose, the lost hikers **subsequently** found the _____ down the hill.

- My sister had initially joined the track team but **subsequently** had to withdraw because she broke her _____ .

Synonyms
- after; later

Antonyms
- before; earlier

Family
- **Adjective:** subsequent

Word Partners
- what subsequently happened
- subsequently became

Examples
- During the night, rain flooded the streets. This explained **what subsequently happened** to traffic the next morning.
- Hollywood produced a popular movie based on a novel about space travel, and the book **subsequently became** a best-seller.

✏ Try It
Our teacher taught us a trick for solving _____ problems, and **subsequently** I got an A on the final math test.

VERBAL PRACTICE

Talk about it

Discuss Listen Write

Discuss ideas with your partner, listen to classmates, and then write your favorite idea.

1. At first the little boy was excited about his new balloon, but **subsequently** he became very sad when the balloon _____ .

2. It was a great day because we were first in line at the ticket booth and **subsequently** discovered that our best friends got the seats next to us at the

_____

68 Unit 4

WRITING PRACTICE

Collaborate

Discuss
Agree
Write
Listen

Discuss ideas with your partner and agree on the best words to complete the frame. ▶

Because our best _____ was injured during the first inning,

no one was surprised that we _____ lost the game.

Our Turn

Discuss
Listen
Write

Read the prompt. Work with the teacher to complete the frames. Write a thoughtful response that includes a convincing reason. ▶

PROMPT: **A high school student was kicked out of a theater but subsequently became a spokesperson for laws that affect children. Read the sequence of events that led to the change.**

The local newspaper _____ that a student had been kicked out of a

theater for paying for one movie but watching more than one. The _____

explained that sneaking into a movie was against the law. The student

_____ volunteered to explain the law to other students.

Be an Academic Author

Write
Discuss
Listen

Read the prompt and complete the frames. Strengthen your response with a relevant example.

PROMPT: **Many animals form and subsequently change. What changes occur in a frog's lifetime?**

First, a female frog lays _____ eggs. Each egg hatches and becomes a tadpole

that uses its tail to swim in a _____ . Over time, a tadpole grows legs, and its tail

_____ disappears. Finally, the adult frog uses its legs to _____ around on land.

Construct a Response

Write
Discuss
Listen

Read the prompt and construct a thoughtful response. Include a convincing reason to strengthen your response. ▶

PROMPT: **If your friend became famous, how would you make sure that the two of you remained friends?**

_____

_____

_____

_____

grammar tip ▶

A **past-tense verb** describes an action that already happened. To write the past tense, add *-ed* to the end of a verb.

EXAMPLE: My friend **repeated** the joke over and over and we all **laughed** again and again.

eventually
adverb

Say it: e • ven • tu • al • ly

Write it: _____

Write it again: _____

_____

Meaning
after a long time, especially after a long delay or many challenges

Synonyms
- finally; at last

Antonyms
- initially; at first

Examples
- It will take weeks, but **eventually** the students will complete the _____ .

- After several complaints about speeding _____ near the school, the city **eventually** installed traffic lights.

Family
- **Adjective:** eventual

Word Partners
- eventually lead/led to

- eventually succeeded

Examples
- The principal's decision to eat lunch with the students **eventually led to** better relationships with the fifth graders.
- After years of research and experimentation, Thomas Edison **eventually succeeded** in creating a functional electric lightbulb.

Try It

Although it took several days, our science team's collaboration **eventually** led to (a/an) _____

_____ display of the solar system.

VERBAL PRACTICE

Talk about it

Discuss
Listen
Write

Discuss ideas with your partner, listen to classmates, and then write your favorite idea.

1. Several classes kept track of their recycling each week, which **eventually** led to a

   reduction in the amount of _____ in the garbage cans.

2. After posting pictures of their unusual pet and telling every neighbor that

   she was missing, the family **eventually** succeeded in finding their beloved

   _____ .

eventually
adverb

WRITING PRACTICE

Collaborate

Discuss
Agree
Write
Listen

Discuss ideas with your partner and agree on the best words to complete the frame. ▶

One year, the fifth graders started a vegetable garden that produced so much

_____ food that the fourth graders decided to a start garden.

Perhaps _____ every grade level will have a garden!

Our Turn

Discuss
Listen
Write

Read the prompt. Work with the teacher to complete the frames. Write a thoughtful response that includes a relevant example. ▶

PROMPT: How could your school conduct a reading contest that eventually benefits your class?

For the contest, our school could ask teachers to _____ the number

of pages students read during free time. After a few weeks, we could ask a publisher to

_____ free books to each classroom. _____ , we could

earn so many books that we'd need more bookshelves for our class library!

Be an Academic Author

Write
Discuss
Listen

Read the prompt and complete the frames. Strengthen your response with a convincing reason.

PROMPT: Think about the water cycle. What eventually happens to all water?

All water is part of an endless cycle. In various bodies of water, such as _____ ,

water evaporates and becomes vapor. The vapor rises and collects in the form of clouds.

When the vapor cools, it condenses and _____ as rain, hail, or snow.

_____ , that water evaporates to restart the cycle.

Construct a Response

Write
Discuss
Listen

Read the prompt and construct a thoughtful response. Include a convincing reason to strengthen your response. ▶

PROMPT: What could you do today that could eventually lead to achieving one of your goals?

_____

_____

_____

grammar tip ▶

Use the **modal verb**, or helping verb, *could* to show that something might be possible. When you use *could*, add a verb in the base form.

EXAMPLE: I bet our old dog **could** learn new tricks if we sent her to obedience school.

ultimately
adverb

Say it: ul • ti • mate • ly

✏️ **Write it:** _____   **Write it again:** _____

🌐 _____

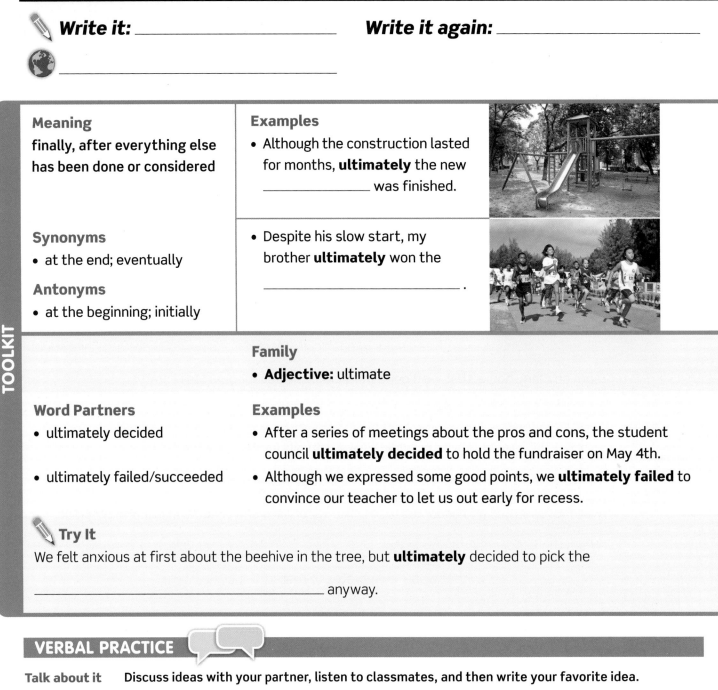

TOOLKIT

Meaning
finally, after everything else has been done or considered

Synonyms
• at the end; eventually

Antonyms
• at the beginning; initially

Examples
• Although the construction lasted for months, **ultimately** the new _____ was finished.

• Despite his slow start, my brother **ultimately** won the _____ .

Family
• **Adjective:** ultimate

Word Partners
• ultimately decided

• ultimately failed/succeeded

Examples
• After a series of meetings about the pros and cons, the student council **ultimately decided** to hold the fundraiser on May 4th.

• Although we expressed some good points, we **ultimately failed** to convince our teacher to let us out early for recess.

✏️ **Try It**
We felt anxious at first about the beehive in the tree, but **ultimately** decided to pick the _____ anyway.

VERBAL PRACTICE 💬

Talk about it

Discuss
Listen
Write

Discuss ideas with your partner, listen to classmates, and then write your favorite idea.

1. While both candidates ran excellent campaigns for student council president, the fifth grader **ultimately** won because she made more _____ promises.

2. My neighbor emphasized that if we played soccer in front of his house, **ultimately** it was our responsibility to repair any broken _____ .

ultimately
adverb

WRITING PRACTICE

Collaborate

Discuss
Agree
Write
Listen

Discuss ideas with your partner and agree on the best words to complete the frame. ▶

For the concert, we had an idea that _____ led to (a/an) _____

_____ , which expressed our understanding of the Underground Railroad.

Our Turn

Discuss
Listen
Write

Read the prompt. Work with the teacher to complete the frames. Write a thoughtful response that includes a convincing reason.

PROMPT: What are rules your class can follow to ultimately create better classroom collaboration?

For better classroom collaboration, use these rules: (1) Share ideas about the

_____ . (2) Listen and think about others' _____ .

(3) Ask and answer questions _____ . The rules may seem

awkward at first, but _____ the outcome will be stronger class discussions.

Be an Academic Author

Write
Discuss
Listen

Read the prompt and complete the frames. Strengthen your response with a convincing reason.

PROMPT: What could you do that will ultimately benefit the lives of children in your community?

To benefit the lives of children in my community, I could collect and

_____ gently used books to local children's hospitals. In

addition, I could read to younger _____ at our school. By

sharing my time, I will _____ have a positive impact on my community.

Construct a Response

Write
Discuss
Listen

Read the prompt and construct a thoughtful response. Include a convincing reason to strengthen your response.

PROMPT: What new skill or talent would you like to develop? Describe what you could do that would ultimately help you develop that new skill or talent.

_____

_____

_____

_____

---

grammar tip ▶

A **past-tense verb** describes an action that already happened. To write the past tense, add *-ed* to the end of a verb.

EXAMPLE: On Saturday, it **rained** all day. So I **stayed** indoors, **watched** TV, and **played** video games.

preceding
adjective

Say it: pre • ced • ing

🖊 **Write it:** _____   **Write it again:** _____

🌐 _____

Meaning	Examples
happening or coming before the event or part that is being discussed	• In **preceding** Olympic Games, Team USA's discus throwers won _____ medals.
Synonyms • earlier **Antonyms** • following	• Because the _____ we held during the **preceding** year was so successful, we decided to have one this year.

Family
• **Verb:** precede

Word Partners
• preceding event(s)

• preceding paragraph(s)/ section(s)/chapter(s)/ page(s)/episode(s)

Examples
• We hope that this year's fundraiser will be as successful as **preceding events**, such as the Spaghetti Feed last year.
• In the **preceding episode** of my favorite T.V. show, two talented singers were voted out of the competition.

🖊 **Try It**

I'm looking forward to today's reading assignment, since the **preceding** chapter ended with the sentence,

"It was unfortunate that he didn't see the aggressive _____ coming his way."

VERBAL PRACTICE

Talk about it   Discuss ideas with your partner, listen to classmates, and then write your favorite idea.

Discuss
Listen
Write

1. The guest speaker announced that she attended the _____

   honoring the best students from our local high school the **preceding** week.

2. My dad was angry that we took the 5:30 bus and got to the _____

   late. If we had taken the **preceding** bus we would have arrived on time.

preceding
adjective

WRITING PRACTICE

Collaborate

Discuss
Agree
Write
Listen

Discuss ideas with your partner and agree on the best words to complete the frame. ▶

We appreciated that our teachers worked hard during the _____

week to prepare for the first day of school by organizing all the _____ .

Our Turn

Discuss
Listen
Write

Read the prompt. Work with the teacher to complete the frames. Write a thoughtful response that includes a convincing reason. ▶

PROMPT: How do preceding events help scientists predict future events?

Scientists can use knowledge of _____ events to predict future

events. By _____ earthquake patterns, seismologists try to

predict when a quake might _____ .

Be an Academic Author

Write
Discuss
Listen

Read the prompt and complete the frames. Strengthen your response with a convincing reason.

PROMPT: Imagine you ripped open a packet of hot chocolate mix and the only visible direction reads "Step (3) Add marshmallows. Enjoy!" What do you think were the preceding directions?

I'm confident the directions _____ Step 3 were (1) Empty

_____ into a cup, and (2) _____

stir in hot water or milk. I am certain about the directions because I've made hot chocolate

_____ times.

Construct a Response

Write
Discuss
Listen

Read the prompt and construct a thoughtful response. Include a convincing reason to strengthen your response. ▶

PROMPT: You walked into the kitchen and discovered garbage strewn everywhere, paw prints along the counter, and a strong odor. What were the preceding events that led to this mess?

_____

_____

_____

_____

_____

grammar tip ▶

Use a **verb + ing** after the prepositions *by, of,* and *for.*

EXAMPLE: By plotting moves in advance, a chess player can anticipate an opponent's moves.

initially

DAY 1

REVIEW: outcome *noun*

Softball games can be exciting, especially when the _____

is determined by the last _____ .

initially *adverb*

DAY 2

We _____ proposed having our

_____ on Friday, but when we saw the

weather forecast, we decided to postpone it to Saturday.

DAY 3

I _____ thought that the TV show

_____ was uninteresting but

then a friend encouraged me to watch a few episodes, and now I like it.

DAY 4

My classmates and I _____ found the

_____ from the '80s very unusual,

but our teacher loves that time period, so we are beginning to understand it.

DAY 5

When I met the new girl, I _____ thought

that she was a snob. After we worked together on a school project, though, I

_____ that she was very friendly and helpful.

TOTAL

SMART START

DAY 1

REVIEW: **initially** *adverb*

A television show that I _____ found confusing

has now become a favorite because my _____

explained the last season to me.

DAY 2

previously *adverb*

_____ , when I was in the fourth grade, I believed

that it was okay to be late. But recently I learned that being late is considered

_____ and bad manners, so now I try to arrive on time.

DAY 3

_____ , people thought that eating

lots of meat and potatoes was a healthy diet. Today, health research has

_____ that people need to eat more vegetables and fruits.

DAY 4

Buying products, such as _____ that (was/

were) _____ _____ owned by someone else, can help

the environment because it reduces the amount of waste that ends up in garbage dumps.

DAY 5

_____ , some of the math games in the school's

computer lab seemed boring. However, now that the software has been upgraded, many

games have exciting new _____ .

TOTAL

subsequently

DAY 1

REVIEW: previously   *adverb*

The story that I had _____

hated became a favorite after I _____ .

☐

☐

DAY 2

subsequently   *adverb*

My uncle agreed to loan me money to buy a gift for my friend's birthday

and _____ I promised to

_____ at his house to pay him back.

☐

☐

DAY 3

I went over to my friend's house to study for the social studies test, and then we

_____ ended up listening to music and playing

_____ .

☐

☐

DAY 4

After our _____ dress rehearsal, no one was surprised by

what _____ happened when the play was a terrific success.

☐

☐

DAY 5

Initially, the magazine article reported that two _____

were in a terrible car crash. However, the magazine _____

issued a correction stating that they were actually nowhere near the accident.

☐

☐

TOTAL

SMARTSTART

DAY 1

REVIEW: **subsequently**   *adverb*

I taught my _____ a lot of tricks, and he

_____ became a star in a

television commercial.

☐
☐

DAY 2

eventually   *adverb*

Getting plenty of exercise and eating a diet that includes vegetables and fruits can

_____ lead to

a healthy body and a _____ mind.

☐
☐

DAY 3

So much rain fell over the weekend that all the _____

in our neighborhood were _____ flooded with water.

☐
☐

DAY 4

After several hours coaching my grandparents to use their new smartphone, they

_____ succeeded in sending a few

_____ to my brother who is away at college.

☐
☐

DAY 5

Many teachers realize that gentle reminders about rules and expectations will

_____ lead to an orderly and

_____ classroom environment.

☐
☐

TOTAL

ultimately

 SMART *START*

REVIEW: eventually   *adverb*

 DAY 1

Despite many disagreements, the students _____

completed a list of favorite snacks and refreshments to serve at the end-of-year

☐

_____ .

☐

---

ultimately   *adverb*

DAY 2

Although the hike along a narrow path, through tall grasses and prickly bushes, was

_____ for the hiker, she _____

☐

achieved her goal of being the first blind person to reach the mountain's highest peak.

☐

DAY 3

The town council was _____ able to allocate enough

☐

money to build a new _____ near the city hall.

☐

 DAY 4

Even though my team worked for many hours, we _____

failed to finish our _____ project on time

☐

and had to ask our teacher for an extension.

☐

 DAY 5

During my month-long research about ants, I initially thought I would just

_____ about their physical

traits, but I _____ learned more about ant behavior

☐

and their sense of cooperation and community.

☐

TOTAL

⚑ SMART START

DAY 1

REVIEW: **ultimately** *adverb*

Even though it seemed impossible at first, the astronauts _____

managed to repair the damaged _____

and the mission continued successfully.

preceding *adjective*

DAY 2

I brought extra pencils to the student council meeting today because one student

_____ has forgotten to

bring a pencil during the _____ meetings.

DAY 3

Our _____ arrived an

hour late because their _____ flight was

delayed due to bad weather.

DAY 4

My best friend had been in a _____

mood the _____ week because

she heard a rumor that I was moving to New York.

DAY 5

Sometimes what you learned from a _____

experience can help you solve current _____ .

TOTAL

Create

Create means to make something.

To **create** a plan, solution, or an explanation you need to think carefully and consider different ways to answer a question.

To **create** stories, poems, and other pieces of writing you need to use your imagination and explore many ideas.

Find It Read the sample tasks below and circle the steps that would help you **create** a strong response.

1. Think about the story of Hansel and Gretel and write a different ending.

   a. Review the plot and think of way for Hansel, Gretel, and the witch to become friends.
   b. Change the setting of the witch's house.
   c. Include a puppy named Sparky.

2. Explain how litter affects the environment. Include two details to support your answer.

   a. Think of two ways that litter negatively affects the environment.
   b. Write about litter at your school.
   c. Write about the importance of recycling.

Try It **Create** a plan to convince your parents/guardians to let you have a cell phone.

Reasons Why Students Should _____ **a Cell Phone**

1. Cell phones are _____ in emergencies.

2. The free or inexpensive apps _____ entertainment for kids.

3. Cells phones can help encourage children to _____ .

4. It's (a/an) _____ _____ way of communicating.

5. Cell phones can help parents or guardians _____ their children.

RATE WORD KNOWLEDGE

Circle the number that shows your knowledge of the words you'll use as you create plans, solutions, stories, poems, and other pieces of writing.

3rd Grade	4th Grade	BEFORE	5th Grade	AFTER
complete	present	1 2 3 4	**produce**	1 2 3 4
task	develop	1 2 3 4	**propose**	1 2 3 4
prepare	provide	1 2 3 4	**collaborate**	1 2 3 4
provide	revise	1 2 3 4	**accomplish**	1 2 3 4
organize	demonstrate	1 2 3 4	**create**	1 2 3 4
response	elaborate	1 2 3 4	**strategy**	1 2 3 4

RATE IT

DISCUSSION GUIDE
- Form groups of four.
- Assign letters to each person. Ⓐ Ⓑ Ⓓ Ⓒ
- Each group member takes a turn leading a discussion.
- Prepare to report about one word.

DISCUSS WORDS

Discuss how well you know the fifth grade words. Then, report to the class how you rated each word.

GROUP LEADER **Ask**

So, _____ what do you know
　　　　(NAME)

about the word _____ ?

GROUP MEMBERS **Discuss**

1 = I **don't recognize** the word _____ .

I need to learn what it means.

2 = I **recognize** the word _____ ,

but I need to learn the meaning.

3 = I'm **familiar** with the word _____ .

I think it means _____ .

4 = I **know** the word _____ .

It's a _____ , and it means _____ .
　　　　(PART OF SPEECH)

Here is my example sentence: _____ .

REPORTER **Report Word Knowledge**

Our group gave the word _____ a rating of _____ because _____ .

SET A GOAL AND REFLECT

First, set a vocabulary goal for this unit by selecting at least three words that you plan to thoroughly learn. At the end of the unit, return to this page and write a reflection about one word you have mastered.

GOAL

During this unit I plan to thoroughly learn the words _____ ,

_____ , and _____ . Increasing my word knowledge will

help me speak and write effectively when I create plans and _____ .

As a result of this unit, I feel most confident about the word _____ .

This is my model sentence: _____

_____ .

REFLECTION

produce
verb

✏️ **Write it:** _____ **Write it again:** _____

🌐 _____

TOOLKIT

Meaning
to make or create something

Synonyms
• make; invent

Examples
• All you need are colorful
_____ and a string
to **produce** beautiful necklaces.

• Skunks **produce** a
_____ odor when
they are frightened and want to
defend themselves.

Forms
• **Present:**
  I/You/We/They produce
  He/She/It   produces
• **Past:**   produced

Family
• **Noun:** product
• **Adjective:** productive

Word Partners
• produce an original
  (poem, play, etc.)
• able/unable to produce

Examples
• When I was in second grade, my class **produced an original** play
  about pirates that we performed for the school.
• If we don't buy more butter from the store now, we will be **unable
  to produce** enough cookies for the bake sale tomorrow.

✏️ **Try It**
The factory was unable to **produce** _____ quickly enough, which led to it closing down.

VERBAL PRACTICE 💬

Talk about it

**Discuss
Listen
Write**

Discuss ideas with your partner, listen to classmates, and then write your favorite idea.

1. Our teacher often asks us to **produce** original _____ based on
   our personal experiences.

2. If I have enough time to _____, I will be able to
   produce a great report for school.

WRITING PRACTICE

Collaborate

Discuss
Agree
Write
Listen

Discuss ideas with your partner and agree on the best words to complete the frame. ▶

If you take excellent care of a garden, it will _____ wonderful

_____ .

Our Turn

Discuss
Listen
Write

Read the prompt. Work with the teacher to complete the frames. Write a thoughtful response that includes a convincing reason.

PROMPT: Think about a time when you weren't able to produce the correct answers on a test. Why did that happen?

I usually try to do my best, but I was once unable to _____ the

correct answers on a _____ test. This happened because I didn't

_____ before the test.

Be an Academic Author

Write
Discuss
Listen

Read the prompt and complete the frames. Strengthen your response with a personal experience. ▶

PROMPT: If you practice something difficult every day, what type of results will you be able to produce over time?

By practicing something difficult every day, you will be able to _____

some _____ results over time. Personally, I learned how to

_____ very well by working at it just a little bit every day.

Construct a Response

Write
Discuss
Listen

Read the prompt and construct a thoughtful response. Include a convincing reason to strengthen your response.

PROMPT: Think about a time you produced an original craft, piece of art, or piece of writing that you were very proud of. Why did it make you proud?

_____

_____

_____

_____

grammar tip ▶

A **future tense verb** tells what will happen later, or in the future. To write the future tense, add the word *will* before the base verb.

EXAMPLE: I *will have* my next birthday party at a bowling alley, and all of my friends and cousins *will be* there.

propose
verb

Say it: pro • pose

✏️ **Write it:** _____   **Write it again:** _____

🌐 _____

Meaning to offer ideas about something	**Examples** • All the students were _____ to **propose** an idea for a game to play in class.	
Synonyms • suggest	• Some parents in the neighborhood proposed a plan for a new _____ in the local park.	

TOOLKIT

Forms
• **Present:**
I/You/We/They	propose
He/She/It	proposes
• **Past:**   proposed

Family
• **Noun:** proposal

Word Partners
• propose a/an (topic/idea/ plan)
• propose (a few/some) changes

Examples
• I couldn't think of what to write my English essay about, so my teacher **proposed a topic** for me.
• When the teenager brought home a bad report card, his mother **proposed some changes** to his study habits.

✏️ **Try It**

It was great weather on Saturday, so I **proposed** an idea for a _____ .

VERBAL PRACTICE 💬

Talk about it

Discuss
Listen
Write

Discuss ideas with your partner, listen to classmates, and then write your favorite idea.

1. My brother and I didn't think that the plans for our family's _____

sounded that interesting, so we **proposed** a few changes.

2. If I had to **propose** a science topic for us to study, I'd suggest we learn about

_____ .

propose
verb

WRITING PRACTICE

Collaborate

Discuss
Agree
Write
Listen

Discuss ideas with your partner and agree on the best words to complete the frame. ▶

Recently, we _____ fun ideas for the class field trip, such as a

trip to the _____ or to the _____ .

Our Turn

Discuss
Listen
Write

Read the prompt. Work with the teacher to complete the frames. Write a thoughtful response that includes a personal experience. ▶

PROMPT: Things don't always go the way we plan them. Tell about a time when you had to propose a new plan because something went wrong.

Last week my friend and I had plans to _____ ,

but we couldn't because of bad weather. So I _____

a plan to stay in and _____ instead.

Be an Academic Author

Write
Discuss
Listen

Read the prompt and complete the frames. Strengthen your response with a relevant example.

PROMPT: What changes to the cafeteria menu would you propose if you had the opportunity?

If I could _____ changes to the school cafeteria menu, I would ask

for more _____ options. For example, I'd love

to have _____ sometimes.

Construct a Response

Write
Discuss
Listen

Read the prompt and construct a thoughtful response. Include a personal experience to strengthen your response. ▶

PROMPT: Think of a time when you proposed an idea or solution that helped solve a problem. What was the problem, and what solution did you propose?

_____

_____

_____

_____

grammar tip ▶

A **past-tense verb** describes an action that already happened. For verbs that end in silent *e*, drop the final *e* before you add *-ed*.

EXAMPLE: My parents **decided** that they **liked** the blue wallpaper better than the green.

collaborate
verb

Say it: col • la • bo • rate

✏️ **Write it:** _____   **Write it again:** _____

🌐 _____

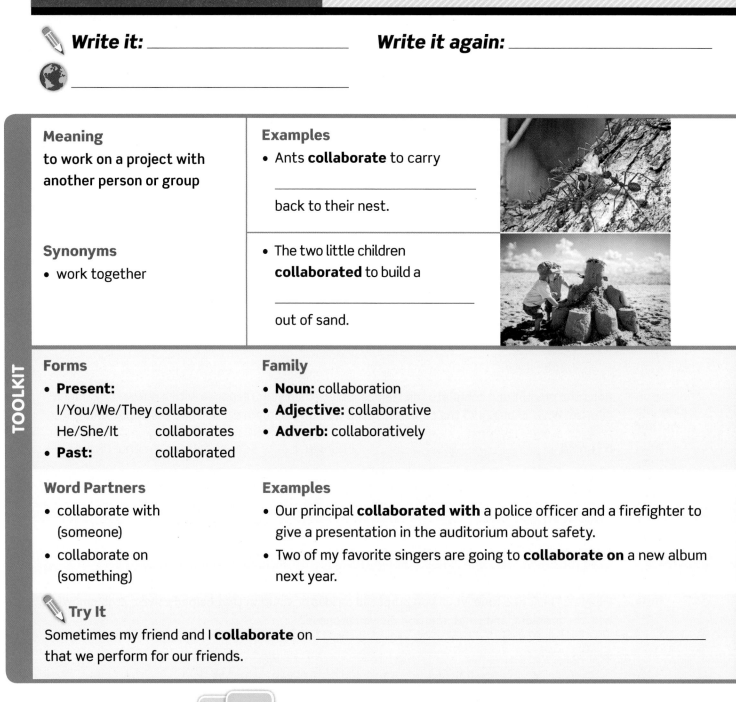

Meaning to work on a project with another person or group	**Examples** • Ants **collaborate** to carry _____ back to their nest.
Synonyms • work together	• The two little children **collaborated** to build a _____ out of sand.

TOOLKIT

Forms
- **Present:**
  I/You/We/They collaborate
  He/She/It   collaborates
- **Past:**   collaborated

Family
- **Noun:** collaboration
- **Adjective:** collaborative
- **Adverb:** collaboratively

Word Partners
- collaborate with (someone)
- collaborate on (something)

Examples
- Our principal **collaborated with** a police officer and a firefighter to give a presentation in the auditorium about safety.
- Two of my favorite singers are going to **collaborate on** a new album next year.

✏️ **Try It**

Sometimes my friend and I **collaborate** on _____ that we perform for our friends.

VERBAL PRACTICE 💬

Talk about it   Discuss ideas with your partner, listen to classmates, and then write your favorite idea.

> **Discuss**
> **Listen**
> **Write**

1. My friends and I **collaborated** to make a big pasta dinner with salad. I was in charge of _____ .

2. If you and a partner are on the same team in a competition such as a _____ _____ , you need to **collaborate** with each other.

collaborate
verb

Collaborate

Discuss
Agree
Write
Listen

Discuss ideas with your partner and agree on the best words to complete the frame. ▶

After we read the _____ text in class, we're going to get into small

groups and _____ with each other to answer questions about it.

Our Turn

Discuss
Listen
Write

Read the prompt. Work with the teacher to complete the frames. Write a thoughtful response that includes a relevant example.

PROMPT: **Why is it often helpful to collaborate with someone on a difficult task?**

It is often helpful to _____ with someone on a difficult task because

this makes the task _____ to accomplish. For example, if you have

to set up a _____ for a big _____, you'll

accomplish more and in less time by working with others.

Be an Academic Author

Write
Discuss
Listen

Read the prompt and complete the frames. Strengthen your response with a convincing reason. ▶

PROMPT: **Imagine you and a friend are going to collaborate on a birthday card for your teacher. What tasks are each of you going to complete and why?**

I'm going to _____ with my friend on a birthday card for our teacher. I'm a strong

_____ so I plan to _____

on the cover. On the inside, my friend is going to write (a/an) _____

_____ because my friend is a creative writer.

Construct a Response

Write
Discuss
Listen

Read the prompt and construct a thoughtful response. Include a relevant example to strengthen your response.

PROMPT: **In many books and movies, the main character collaborates with other characters to achieve a goal. Can you think of one example?**

_____

_____

_____

grammar tip ▶

A **future tense verb** tells what will happen later, or in the future. To write the future tense, add the phrase am going to, is going to, or are going to before the base verb.

EXAMPLE: We **are going to do** test prep tomorrow. Then we **are going to take** the test on Friday.

accomplish
verb

Say it: ac • **com** • plish

✏️ **Write it:** _____ **Write it again:** _____

🌐 _____

Meaning	**Examples**
to succeed in doing something special or challenging	• The young girl is finally **accomplishing** her goal of learning to ride a _____ .

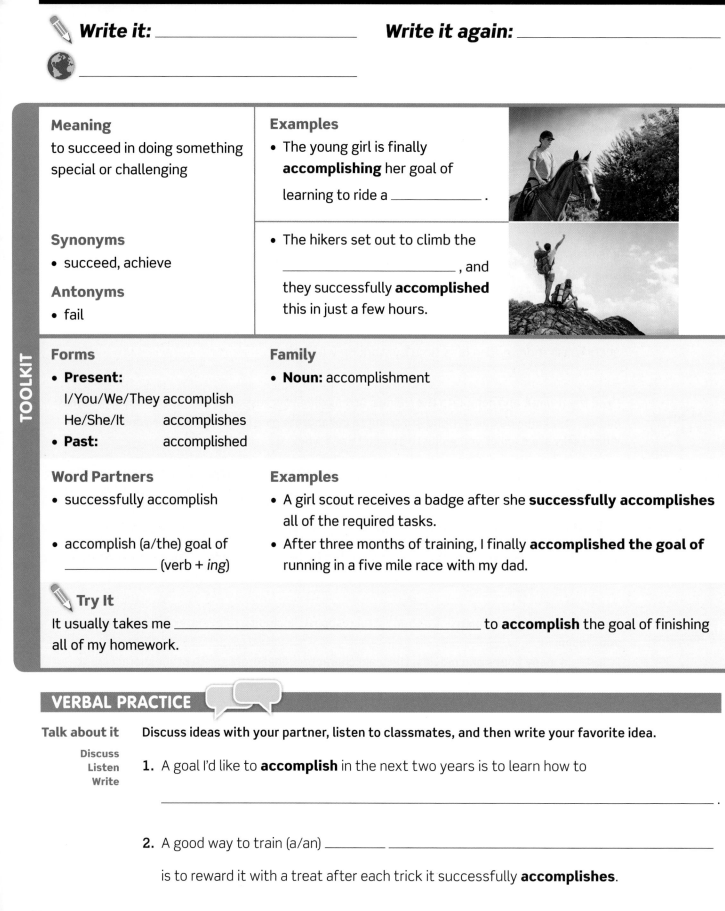

	Examples
Synonyms • succeed, achieve **Antonyms** • fail	• The hikers set out to climb the _____ , and they successfully **accomplished** this in just a few hours.

Forms
- **Present:**
  I/You/We/They accomplish
  He/She/It   accomplishes
- **Past:**   accomplished

Family
- **Noun:** accomplishment

Word Partners
- successfully accomplish

- accomplish (a/the) goal of
  _____ (verb + *ing*)

Examples
- A girl scout receives a badge after she **successfully accomplishes** all of the required tasks.
- After three months of training, I finally **accomplished the goal of** running in a five mile race with my dad.

✏️ **Try It**

It usually takes me _____ to **accomplish** the goal of finishing all of my homework.

VERBAL PRACTICE 💬

Talk about it

Discuss
Listen
Write

Discuss ideas with your partner, listen to classmates, and then write your favorite idea.

1. A goal I'd like to **accomplish** in the next two years is to learn how to

_____ .

2. A good way to train (a/an) _____ _____

is to reward it with a treat after each trick it successfully **accomplishes**.

WRITING PRACTICE

Collaborate

Discuss
Agree
Write
Listen

Discuss ideas with your partner and agree on the best words to complete the frame. ▶

A child who successfully _____ all of his chores at home should

receive (a/an) _____ from his parents.

Our Turn

Discuss
Listen
Write

Read the prompt. Work with the teacher to complete the frames. Write a thoughtful response that includes a personal experience.

PROMPT: You learn different things, or have different learning goals, in each school subject. What is one goal you and your classmates successfully accomplished in math this year?

In math this year, we successfully _____ the goal of

learning how to _____ . For

me, it was very _____ to learn.

Be an Academic Author

Write
Discuss
Listen

Read the prompt and complete the frames. Strengthen your response with a personal experience. ▶

PROMPT: How does a person feel when he or she successfully accomplishes something challenging? Think of something difficult you accomplished recently. How did you feel?

A person usually feels _____ when he or she successfully

_____ something challenging. Personally, I finished working

on (a/an) _____ recently for my

_____ , and it was a really great feeling.

Construct a Response

Write
Discuss
Listen

Read the prompt and construct a thoughtful response. Include a personal experience to strengthen your response.

PROMPT: It's important to set goals for yourself. Think about one goal you want to accomplish sometime soon. How do you plan to achieve this goal?

_____

_____

_____

_____

grammar tip ▶

A **present tense verb** describes an action that happens usually, sometimes, or never. For verbs that end in *x*, *ch*, *sh*, *ss*, or *z*, add **-es** to the end of the verb.

EXAMPLE: My grandmother in Russia **misses** us and **wishes** she could see us more often.

create
verb

Say it: cre • ate

Write it: _____   Write it again: _____

_____

TOOLKIT

Meaning
to make something new

Examples
- Some artists **create** sculptures out of _____ .

- There is a _____ in the tree behind our house that was **created** by birds.

Synonyms
- make

Forms
- **Present:**

  I/You/We/They   create

  He/She/It   creates
- **Past:**   created

Family
- **Noun:** creativity
- **Adjective:** creative
- **Adverb:** creatively

Word Partners
- to be created by

- create a (plan, outline)

Examples
- The huge puddles in front of my house **were created by** a powerful rain storm last night.
- Before building a dollhouse for his daughter, the father **created a plan** using paper and pencil.

✏️ Try It
Before you write (a/an) _____ _____ ,
it's helpful to **create** an outline using your notes.

VERBAL PRACTICE

Talk about it   Discuss ideas with your partner, listen to classmates, and then write your favorite idea.

Discuss
Listen
Write

1. Using colored paper, glue, markers, and scissors, my friends and I will **create** some

   _____ for the party.

2. Several neighborhood children and I got together and **created** a plan for building (a/an)

   _____ _____ in my backyard.

create
verb

WRITING PRACTICE

Collaborate

Discuss
Agree
Write
Listen

Discuss ideas with your partner and agree on the best words to complete the frame. ▶

Before we celebrated _____ ,

we _____ a plan for the celebration, including a list of the

_____ we needed to buy.

Our Turn

Discuss
Listen
Write

Read the prompt. Work with the teacher to complete the frames. Write a thoughtful response that includes a convincing reason. ▶

PROMPT: **People aren't the only ones who create things. Animals create things too! Think of something you've seen around your neighborhood that animals created. What is it, and why do animals create it?**

In my neighborhood, you can find many _____ that were

_____ by _____ .

The animals make these so that they can _____ .

Be an Academic Author

Write
Discuss
Listen

Read the prompt and complete the frames. Strengthen your response with a personal experience. ▶

PROMPT: **Think about a time when you created a mess in your kitchen or living room. What were you doing that caused the mess and what did you do to clean up afterward?**

Once, I _____ a mess in the (kitchen/living room)

_____ when I _____

_____ . Afterward,

I cleaned up by _____ .

Construct a Response

Write
Discuss
Listen

Read the prompt and construct a thoughtful response. Include a personal experience to strengthen your response. ▶

PROMPT: **Do you have an object that someone created for you? Describe it. Who gave it to you and why?**

_____

_____

grammar tip ▶

A **past-tense verb** describes an action that already happened. For verbs that end in silent *e*, drop the final *e* before you add *-ed*.

EXAMPLE: The campers **prepared** roasted marshmallow sandwiches with the graham crackers and marshmallows that the camp counselors **provided** for them.

strategy
noun

✏️ **Write it:** _____   **Write it again:** _____

🌐 _____

TOOLKIT

Meaning

a planned way of completing or achieving something

Synonyms

• plan; method

Examples

• To win a game of _____ , you need to develop effective **strategies**.

• The _____ team huddled together with their coach to discuss a **strategy** for their next play.

Forms

• **Singular:** strategy
• **Plural:** strategies

Family

• **Verb:** strategize

Word Partners

• an effective strategy for

• (have/develop) a strategy for

Examples

• If you don't have a kitchen fire extinguisher, **an effective strategy for** putting out a fire in a pan is to put the cover on the pan.

• Our mother **developed a strategy for** getting us to eat more vegetables, which is to add some vegetables to our fruit smoothies.

✏️ **Try It**

An effective **strategy** for waking up early in the morning is to _____
_____ .

VERBAL PRACTICE

Talk about it

Discuss
Listen
Write

Discuss ideas with your partner, listen to classmates, and then write your favorite idea.

1. Sometimes an effective **strategy** for fixing a broken _____

   is finding a how-to video online and following the instructions in the video.

2. My teacher has some effective **strategies** for learning new _____

   which she has shared with us.

strategy

noun

Collaborate

Discuss
Agree
Write
Listen

Discuss ideas with your partner and agree on the best words to complete the frame. ▶

If you want to _____ in school, it's important to develop

_____ for studying and getting all of your work done on time.

Our Turn

Discuss
Listen
Write

Read the prompt. Work with the teacher to complete the frames. Write a thoughtful response that includes a personal experience. ▶

PROMPT: **Staying healthy is important. What are two simple strategies for staying healthy?**

Two simple _____ for staying healthy are

eating plenty of _____ and getting plenty of

_____ . When I do these things, I usually

feel _____ .

Be an Academic Author

Write
Discuss
Listen

Read the prompt and complete the frames. Strengthen your response with a relevant example. ▶

PROMPT: **Preparing for a test can be challenging. Do you have some effective strategies for preparing for a vocabulary test?**

I have several effective _____ for preparing for a vocabulary test.

For example, I make _____ to help me memorize the words and

their definitions. I also ask classmates to _____ with me.

Construct a Response

Write
Discuss
Listen

Read the prompt and construct a thoughtful response. Include a relevant example to strengthen your response.

PROMPT: **Knowing how to develop new friendships is an important skill. What is one effective strategy for meeting new people and making new friends?**

_____

_____

_____

_____

grammar tip ▶

Count nouns name things that can be counted. Count nouns have two forms, singular and plural. When count nouns end in a consonant + **-y**, drop the **-y** and add **-ies**.

EXAMPLE: A mother goat can recognize the **cries** of her own **babies**.

produce

REVIEW: preceding *adjective*

DAY 1

Before we watched this week's episode of

_____ ,

I explained to my friend what had happened in the _____

episode.

produce *verb*

DAY 2

When we learn new vocabulary words, our teacher usually asks us to

_____ an original _____

using the words.

DAY 3

If I learned how to sew, I'd be able to _____ my own

_____ .

DAY 4

Last year, our class _____ an original play about

_____ .

DAY 5

A dairy cow _____ milk and cream, which farmers can use to

make _____ .

TOTAL

 **SMART** START

DAY 1

REVIEW: produce   *verb*

Some trees _____ things we can eat, such as

_____ .

☐
☐

DAY 2

propose   *verb*

If I could _____ an idea for an Earth Day project at my

school, it would be to _____

_____ .

☐
☐

DAY 3

While playing a game of _____ outside, I

_____ some changes to the rules to make it a little harder

to win.

☐
☐

DAY 4

The weather was cold but my friend was wearing _____ , so

I _____ he change into warmer clothes before we went outside.

☐
☐

DAY 5

When I stained the bottom of my white shirt with _____

at a restaurant, my mother _____ that I tuck the bottom of

the shirt into my pants so the stain wouldn't show.

☐
☐

TOTAL

collaborate

REVIEW: **propose**   *verb*

DAY 1

Using a pen with red ink, my teacher _____ many changes

to the grammar and _____ in my report.

collaborate   *verb*

DAY 2

Some neighborhood children _____ with each other

to help an elderly neighbor with her _____ .

DAY 3

My brother is _____ with some of his friends to form a

_____ band, but they haven't figured out what to call the

band yet.

DAY 4

As soon as they arrived at the campsite, the group _____

to set up the _____ .

DAY 5

All the students in the class _____ on a giant

_____ that covered the entire wall near the entrance of

the school.

TOTAL

98

SMART START

REVIEW: collaborate   *verb*

DAY 1

Some class projects are very _____ , so it's important

to _____ with classmates in pairs or small groups to

complete them.

☐

☐

accomplish   *verb*

DAY 2

One goal I hope to _____ when I'm an adult is to

_____ .

☐

☐

DAY 3

Kindergarten teachers have to _____ the important goal

of helping their students learn how to _____ .

☐

☐

DAY 4

I work with my _____ in order to

_____ the task of cleaning up the kitchen after dinner.

☐

☐

DAY 5

One task that I successfully _____ at school today was to

_____ .

☐

☐

TOTAL

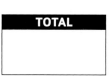

create

SMART START

REVIEW: accomplish *verb*

DAY 1

If I _____ the goal of improving my grades this year, my

parents will get me (a/an) _____ _____ .

create *verb*

DAY 2

Scientists discovered some _____ on the walls of a cave

that prehistoric humans _____ thousands of years ago.

DAY 3

My friends and I _____ a lot of noise while we were

_____ .

DAY 4

Our teacher used a special computer program to _____ a

Web site for our _____ .

DAY 5

A campfire _____ a lot of _____ .

TOTAL

 **SMART** *START*

REVIEW: **create**   *verb*

DAY 1

You can _____ (a/an) _____ _____

with a piece of paper if you know how to fold the paper correctly.

☐
☐

---

strategy   *noun*

DAY 2

One _____ for improving my _____

skills would be to set aside time every day for extra practice.

☐
☐

DAY 3

An effective _____ for understanding new words I see in

(a/an) _____ _____ is to guess the meaning of the

word by looking at the other words around it.

☐
☐

DAY 4

I'd like to develop some _____ for doing my

_____ more quickly and efficiently.

☐
☐

DAY 5

An effective _____ for making sure you get to school on

time in the morning is to _____

_____ .

☐
☐

TOTAL

Compare and Contrast

To **compare** two or more things, analyze what is the same.

To **contrast** two or more things, analyze what is different.

Find It   **Compare** pencils and pens and circle what is the same.

Pencils and Pens

- are used for writing

- use ink

- can be easily erased

Try It   **Contrast** what is different about pencils and pens by adding ideas to each list.

Pencils	Pens
• made of wood	• made of plastic
• make temporary marks	• make permanent marks
• the point or tip needs to be sharpened	• the point or tip doesn't need to be sharpened.
_____	_____

RATE WORD KNOWLEDGE

Circle the number that shows your knowledge of the words you'll use to compare and contrast.

3rd Grade	4th Grade	BEFORE	5th Grade	AFTER
alike	similar	1 2 3 4	**comparison**	1 2 3 4
different	difference	1 2 3 4	**comparable**	1 2 3 4
similar	similarity	1 2 3 4	**contrast**	1 2 3 4
difference	differently	1 2 3 4	**identical**	1 2 3 4
similarity	common	1 2 3 4	**unique**	1 2 3 4
opposite	unlike	1 2 3 4	**differ**	1 2 3 4

RATE IT

DISCUSSION GUIDE
- Form groups of four.
- Assign letters to each person.
- Each group member takes a turn leading a discussion.
- Prepare to report about one word.

Ⓐ Ⓑ
Ⓓ Ⓒ

DISCUSS WORDS

Discuss how well you know the fifth grade words. Then, report to the class how you rated each word.

GROUP LEADER | **Ask**

So, _____ what do you know
     (NAME)

about the word _____ ?

GROUP MEMBERS | **Discuss**

1 = I **don't recognize** the word _____ .

I need to learn what it means.

2 = I **recognize** the word _____ ,

but I need to learn the meaning.

3 = I'm **familiar** with the word _____ .

I think it means _____ .

4 = I **know** the word _____ .

It's a _____ , and it means _____ .
       (PART OF SPEECH)

Here is my example sentence: _____ .

REPORTER | **Report Word Knowledge**

Our group gave the word _____ a rating of _____ because _____ .

SET A GOAL AND REFLECT

First, set a vocabulary goal for this unit by selecting at least three words that you plan to thoroughly learn. At the end of the unit, return to this page and write a reflection about one word you have mastered.

GOAL

During this unit I plan to thoroughly learn the words _____ ,

_____ , and _____ . Increasing my word knowledge will

help me speak and write effectively when I compare and _____ .

As a result of this unit, I feel most confident about the word _____ .

This is my model sentence: _____

_____ .

REFLECTION

comparison

noun

✏️ **Write it:** _____ **Write it again:** _____

🌐 _____

TOOLKIT

Meaning	**Examples**
an explanation about what is the same and what is different between two people or things	• In **comparison** to writing an email or calling someone, _____ is fast and simple. • While shopping for clothes, people usually make **comparisons** between different _____ before deciding what to buy.

Forms
- **Singular:** comparison
- **Plural:** comparisons

Family
- **Verb:** compare
- **Adjective:** comparable

Word Partners
- in comparison to/with
- make a comparison between

Examples
- My brother is quiet **in comparison to** my sister, who is very talkative.
- Before deciding on what kind of pet to get, you should **make a comparison between** the different types of animals and their needs.

✏️ **Try It**

I'm a very _____ person in **comparison** to some children my age.

VERBAL PRACTICE 💬

Talk about it

Discuss
Listen
Write

Discuss ideas with your partner, listen to classmates, and then write your favorite idea.

1. In English class, we often make **comparisons** between texts we've read to find

    similarities and differences between the _____ .

2. In **comparison** with baked potatoes, French fries are _____ .

comparison

noun

WRITING PRACTICE

Collaborate

Discuss
Agree
Write
Listen

Discuss ideas with your partner and agree on the best words to complete the frame. ▷

When your parents are shopping for something expensive, such as (a/an) _____

_____ , they should look for the same item in different stores

to make _____ between the prices.

Our Turn

Discuss
Listen
Write

Read the prompt. Work with the teacher to complete the frames. Write a thoughtful response that includes a personal experience.

PROMPT: Make a comparison between different forms of transportation. Which do you use to get to and from school?

Walking is slow in _____ to other forms of transportation, such as

_____ , but it's good exercise and it's pleasant to have

some time to think and get some fresh air. Personally, I usually _____

to and from school.

Be an Academic Author

Write
Discuss
Listen

Read the prompt and complete the frames. Strengthen your response with a convincing reason.

PROMPT: Compare two of your classes. Why might one be more interesting in comparison to another?

I find my _____ class more interesting in

_____ to my _____ class. This is because I

really enjoy _____ more than anything else.

Construct a Response

Write
Discuss
Listen

Read the prompt and construct a thoughtful response. Include a personal experience to strengthen your response. ▷

PROMPT: We often compare ourselves to others, but this is not usually a good idea. Why should we avoid making comparisons between ourselves and others? What should we do instead?

_____

_____

_____

grammar tip ▷

Use the **modal verb**, or helping verb, *should* to suggest or recommend something. When you use *should*, add a verb in the base form.

You **should** work on your project tonight as it's due at the end of this week.

comparable
adjective

Say it: com • pa• ra• ble

✏️ **Write it:** _____   **Write it again:** _____

🌐 _____

TOOLKIT

Meaning	Examples
fairly similar to another thing so you can easily compare them	• The gray _____ is **comparable** in size to a school bus.

Synonyms
• like; similar to

Antonyms
• unlike; different from

• My father's spaghetti and meatballs is **comparable** to the spaghetti and meatballs at my favorite _____ .

Family
• **Noun:** comparison
• **Verb:** compare

Word Partners
• _____ is comparable in (size, shape, appearance) to
• comparable with

Examples
• Some studies suggest that the African grey parrot **is comparable in intelligence to** a five-year-old child.
• My grandmother's pastries are so elegant that they're actually **comparable with** the ones you can buy in pastry shops.

✏️ **Try It**
The amount of time I spend doing homework every day is **comparable** with the amount of time I spend

_____ .

VERBAL PRACTICE 💬

Talk about it   Discuss ideas with your partner, listen to classmates, and then write your favorite idea.

Discuss
Listen
Write

1. The price of a carton of milk in the cafeteria is **comparable** with the price of (a/an)

_____ .

2. Solving a page of word problems in math is **comparable** in difficulty to

_____ in language arts.

WRITING PRACTICE

Collaborate

Discuss
Agree
Write
Listen

Discuss ideas with your partner and agree on the best words to complete the frame. ▶

I don't think watching a movie on (a/an) _____ _____ is

_____ with watching it on the big screen at a movie theater.

Our Turn

Discuss
Listen
Write

Read the prompt. Work with the teacher to complete the frames. Write a thoughtful response that includes a relevant example. ▶

PROMPT: **Running is a great form of exercise, but not everyone likes to run. What other exercise is comparable to running in the way it benefits your health?**

Everyone should exercise for at least _____ per day to

stay healthy. People who don't like running can do a _____ exercise,

such as _____ .

Be an Academic Author

Write
Discuss
Listen

Read the prompt and complete the frames. Strengthen your response with a personal experience. ▶

PROMPT: **Think about a fun time you had at a restaurant. How could you create a comparable experience at home?**

I had a lot of fun eating at _____ ,

because the food was tasty and I was with my _____ . I could create

a _____ experience at home by inviting the same people and helping

my parents cook similar foods.

Construct a Response

Write
Discuss
Listen

Read the prompt and construct a thoughtful response. Include a personal experience to strengthen your response. ▶

PROMPT: **We often have special relationships with people who share our sense of humor. Who has a sense of humor that is comparable with your own?**

_____

_____

_____

_____

grammar tip ▶

An **adjective** describes, or tells about, a noun. An adjective sometimes appears after verbs such as *is, are, look, feel, smell,* and *taste.*

EXAMPLE: Raccoons may **look cute**, but they **are dangerous** when they **feel trapped.**

contrast

noun

✏️ **Write it:** _____   **Write it again:** _____

🌐 _____

Meaning

a difference between two people or things

Synonyms

- difference; unlike

Antonyms

- similarity

Examples

- There is sometimes a strong **contrast** between the _____ of a house and its door.

- In contrast to _____ , bicycles do not create any pollution.

Forms

- **Singular:** contrast
- **Plural:** contrasts

Word Partners

- in contrast to
- a (clear/strong) contrast between

Family

- **Adjective:** contrasting
- **Verb:** contrast

Examples

- **In contrast to** my diet, my friend eats more fruits and vegetables.
- There is **a clear contrast between** the math concepts I am learning in fifth grade and the math concepts my little brother is learning in second grade.

✏️ **Try It**

In **contrast** to sweet snacks like chocolate, _____ are salty.

VERBAL PRACTICE

Talk about it

Discuss
Listen
Write

Discuss ideas with your partner, listen to classmates, and then write your favorite idea.

1. There are several clear **contrasts** between rock music and _____ .

2. In **contrast** to dogs or cats, _____ would not make very good house pets.

contrast
noun

WRITING PRACTICE

Collaborate

Discuss
Agree
Write
Listen

Discuss ideas with your partner and agree on the best words to complete the frame. ▷

On a sunny day, you can play outside in the park. In _____ , on a rainy

day, you can spend time at (a/an) _____ _____ .

Our Turn

Discuss
Listen
Write

Read the prompt. Work with the teacher to complete the frames. Write a thoughtful response that includes a relevant example. ▷

PROMPT: Yoga is a popular physical activity for people of all ages. What is one clear contrast between yoga and other types of physical activity, such as running, biking, or basketball?

One clear _____ between yoga and many other physical activities is

that yoga is very _____ . Instead of moving quickly and getting out

of breath, you stay in one position for a long period of time. It can be very challenging for

your _____ .

Be an Academic Author

Write
Discuss
Listen

Read the prompt and complete the frames. Strengthen your response with a convincing reason. ▷

PROMPT: Think of one contrast between staying in a hotel or camping in a tent during vacation. Which do you prefer?

In _____ to sleeping in a tent outdoors, staying in a hotel is very

_____ . Personally, I prefer _____ because I

like the feeling of being in (a/an) _____ _____ .

Construct a Response

Write
Discuss
Listen

Read the prompt and construct a thoughtful response. Include a convincing reason to strengthen your response. ▷

PROMPT: Think of two types of jobs that are very different from one another, such as an actor and a scientist. Explain one strong contrast between the jobs. Which job do you think would be a better job for you and why?

_____

_____

_____

_____

grammar tip ▷

A **common noun** names a person, place, thing, or idea. **Singular nouns** name one person, place, thing, or idea. The words *a, an,* and *the* often appear before a singular noun.

EXAMPLE: There is **a difference** between **the water** from **a faucet** and the water from **a natural spring**.

identical

adjective

Say it: i • den ti • cal

Write it: _____   **Write it again:** _____

_____

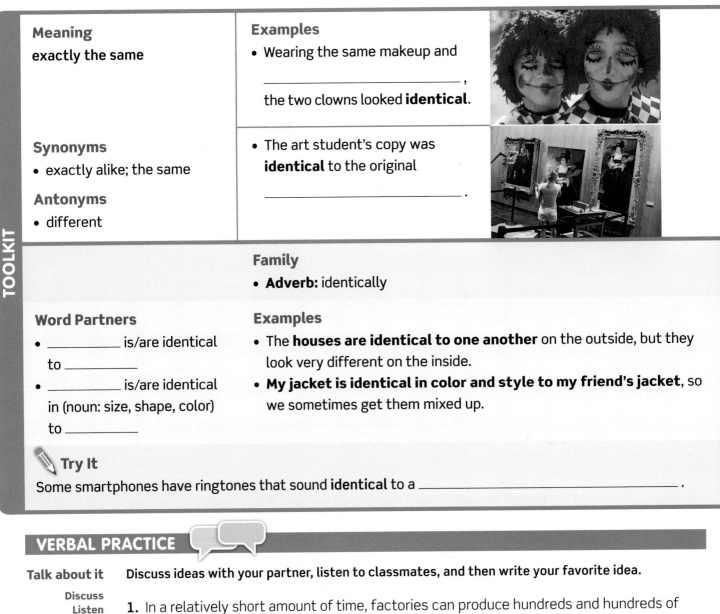

TOOLKIT

Meaning	Examples
exactly the same	• Wearing the same makeup and _____ , the two clowns looked **identical**.
Synonyms • exactly alike; the same **Antonyms** • different	• The art student's copy was **identical** to the original _____ .

Family
• **Adverb:** identically

Word Partners

• _____ is/are identical to _____

• _____ is/are identical in (noun: size, shape, color) to _____

Examples

• The **houses are identical to one another** on the outside, but they look very different on the inside.
• **My jacket is identical in color and style to my friend's jacket**, so we sometimes get them mixed up.

Try It
Some smartphones have ringtones that sound **identical** to a _____ .

VERBAL PRACTICE

Talk about it   Discuss ideas with your partner, listen to classmates, and then write your favorite idea.

Discuss
Listen
Write

1. In a relatively short amount of time, factories can produce hundreds and hundreds of _____ that are **identical** in size, shape, and color.

2. **Identical** twins look exactly alike but can have very different _____ .

WRITING PRACTICE

Collaborate

Discuss
Agree
Write
Listen

Discuss ideas with your partner and agree on the best words to complete the frame. ▶

Feeling compassion for others is important. It means _____

_____ others, even if you've never been in an

_____ situation yourself.

Our Turn

Discuss
Listen
Write

Read the prompt. Work with the teacher to complete the frames. Write a thoughtful response that includes a relevant example. ▶

PROMPT: Sometimes friends have identical opinions about something such as a book, a movie, or a singer. What opinion do you have that's identical to an opinion your friend has?

My friend and I have _____ opinions about _____

_____ . We both think (he/she/it) _____

is _____ and _____ .

Be an Academic Author

Write
Discuss
Listen

Read the prompt and complete the frames. Strengthen your response with a convincing reason. ▶

PROMPT: Things aren't always what they seem in nature. Why do some animals have an identical appearance to other animals or objects in their environment?

Many animals look _____ in color and shape to something else

in their environment, such as a _____ because this is how the

animals avoid being _____ by predators.

Construct a Response

Write
Discuss
Listen

Read the prompt and construct a thoughtful response. Include a relevant example to strengthen your response. ▶

PROMPT: You're different from everyone else in so many ways, but what physical characteristic or personality trait do you have that is identical, or almost identical, to someone else's?

_____

_____

_____

_____

grammar tip ▶

An **adjective** describes, or tells about, a noun. An adjective sometimes appears after verbs such as *is, are, look, feel, smell,* and *taste.*

EXAMPLE: Many cheeses smell **terrible** but taste **delicious**.

unique

adjective

Say it: u • nique

✏️ **Write it:** _____   **Write it again:** _____

🌐 _____

TOOLKIT

Meaning
extremely special and different from other people and things

Synonyms
• special

Antonyms
• ordinary

Examples
• Each _____ is totally unique; no single one is like any other.

• All the pottery we made in art class is unique; each piece was shaped and _____ by hand.

Family
• **Noun:** uniqueness
• **Adverb:** uniquely

Word Partners
• quite unique
• unique to _____

Examples
• My great grandmother's wedding ring is **quite unique**; I've never seen another one like it.
• We used to think that using tools was a characteristic **unique to humans**, but we now know that many other species also use tools.

✏️ **Try It**
What makes me quite **unique** among my friends is my ability to _____ really well.

VERBAL PRACTICE 💬

Talk about it   Discuss ideas with your partner, listen to classmates, and then write your favorite idea.

Discuss
Listen
Write

1. Many famous singers and athletes have **unique** _____ that are created just for them.

2. Living underwater and having _____ are some characteristics **unique** to fish.

WRITING PRACTICE

Collaborate

Discuss
Agree
Write
Listen

Discuss ideas with your partner and agree on the best words to complete the frame. ▶

Many people think the movie star _____

is very special. In particular, this celebrity's ability to _____

is quite unique.

Our Turn

Discuss
Listen
Write

Read the prompt. Work with the teacher to complete the frames. Write a thoughtful response that includes a convincing reason. ▶
PROMPT: **Many schools have an event that is unique to that school. Think of an event that happens at your school each year. What makes your school's event unique?**

Every year, my school has an event called the _____ .

I think my school's event is _____ because I don't

know any other school that has it. This event is special because during it, students

_____ .

Be an Academic Author

Write
Discuss
Listen

Read the prompt and complete the frames. Strengthen your response with a relevant example.
PROMPT: **Think about a holiday that you celebrate. What traditions are unique to that day?**

I enjoy celebrating _____ every year. One tradition

that is _____ to this day is the custom of

_____ .

Construct a Response

Write
Discuss
Listen

Read the prompt and construct a thoughtful response. Include a convincing reason to strengthen your response. ▶
PROMPT: **Think about your favorite place to spend time when you're not at home or at school. What makes this place so unique?**

_____

_____

_____

---

grammar tip ▶

A **possessive noun** shows ownership. Possessive nouns always have apostrophes. For one owner, add *'s* to a singular noun. For more than one owner, keep the *s* at the end of the plural word and add an apostrophe (') at the end.

EXAMPLE: Boys' birthday parties can be loud, but my **brother's** party was calm and fun.

differ
verb

Say it: dif • fer

✏️ **Write it:** _____ **Write it again:** _____

🌐 _____

Meaning
to be different from someone or something else

Synonyms
• contrast

Antonyms
• to be alike

Examples
• An elephant and a _____ **differ** greatly in size.

• The _____ we have today **differ** greatly from the phones of 100 years ago.

Forms
• **Present:**
I/You/We/They   differ
He/She/It   differs
• **Past:**   differed

Family
• **Noun:** difference
• **Adjective:** different
• **Adverb:** differently

Word Partners
• differ from
• differ widely/greatly

Examples
• E-books **differ from** paper books in that you can read them on a screen and carry hundreds of them around with you on your tablet or computer.
• Clothes and hair fashions can **differ greatly** from year to year.

✏️ **Try It**
One way in which sneakers **differ** from flip-flops is that you can _____ with sneakers on.

VERBAL PRACTICE

Talk about it   Discuss ideas with your partner, listen to classmates, and then write your favorite idea.

Discuss
Listen
Write

1. My taste in music **differs** widely from my grandparents'. They usually listen to classical or jazz, while I prefer _____ music.

2. A plant-eating animal's diet of _____ **differs** greatly from the diet of a meat-eating animal.

WRITING PRACTICE

Collaborate

Discuss
Agree
Write
Listen

Discuss ideas with your partner and agree on the best words to complete the frame. ▶

Bulls _____ from cows in many ways. For example, bulls have

sharp horns and are _____ while cows can produce milk and

are _____ .

Our Turn

Discuss
Listen
Write

Read the prompt. Work with the teacher to complete the frames. Write a thoughtful response that includes a relevant example. ▶
PROMPT: **Weekends are a special time. How do your weekends differ from your weekdays?**

My weekend activities _____ greatly from my weekday

activities. For example, on weekdays I have to get up early, go to school, and do homework,

but on weekends, I can _____ .

Be an Academic Author

Write
Discuss
Listen

Read the prompt and complete the frames. Strengthen your response with a relevant example.
PROMPT: **Each country has its own special foods that are popular in that country. How do typical American foods differ from the typical foods in another country?**

Typical American foods _____ greatly from typical

_____ foods. For example, in the United States, foods like pizza,

hamburgers, and macaroni and cheese are popular, but in _____ ,

people enjoy eating _____ .

Construct a Response

Write
Discuss
Listen

Read the prompt and construct a thoughtful response. Include a relevant example to strengthen your response. ▶
PROMPT: **We can't always agree with our friends about everything. How do your opinions differ from your friend's opinions on a certain topic?**

_____

_____

_____

grammar tip ▶

Use the **modal verb**, or helping verb, *can* to show someone is able to do something. When you use *can*, add a verb in the base form.

EXAMPLE: Penguins **can't** fly, but they **can** swim very well.

comparison

REVIEW: strategy   *noun*

DAY 1

One _____ for getting a puppy to go into its crate at night is to

put a _____ into the crate.

☐

☐

comparison   *noun*

DAY 2

In _____ to other cats, my cat is much

_____ .

☐

☐

DAY 3

By making a _____ between last year's

report card and this year's report card, Ellen can see how much her grades

_____ .

☐

☐

DAY 4

It's fun to make some _____ between photos

of myself now and photos of myself when I was little, because I can see how much

_____ I was then.

☐

☐

DAY 5

A cat isn't a very large animal, but in _____ to (a/an)

_____ _____ , it's enormous.

☐

☐

TOTAL

REVIEW: comparison   *noun*

DAY 1

Buying a new car is quite expensive in _____ to buying

a _____ .

☐
☐

---

comparable   *adjective*

DAY 2

An orange is _____ in size to (a/an) _____

_____ .

☐
☐

DAY 3

When it comes to afternoon snacks, walnuts are _____ in health

benefits to _____ .

☐
☐

DAY 4

I lost my favorite _____ last year and haven't been able to

find another that is _____ with it.

☐
☐

DAY 5

Drinking soda is _____ to eating _____

— you're much better off with plain water or milk!

☐
☐

TOTAL

contrast

REVIEW: comparable   *adjective*

DAY 1

When it comes to lunch foods, pizza is _____ in popularity to

_____

among young people in the United States.

---

contrast   *noun*

DAY 2

There is a strong _____ between the color of the walls in my

room and the color of my _____ .

DAY 3

In _____ to many of my friends, I usually _____

_____ after I get home from school.

DAY 4

A field trip to (a/an) _____ _____ would

be fun and exciting in _____ to our usual, ordinary school days.

DAY 5

There is a clear _____ between a news program on TV, which is

meant to inform, and (a/an) _____ _____

show, which is meant to entertain.

TOTAL

118

SMART START

DAY 1

REVIEW: **contrast** *noun*

In _____ to first-graders, fifth-graders are much more

_____ .

☐
☐

DAY 2

identical *adjective*

Our softball uniforms are all _____ in color and style, but we

each wear different _____ .

☐
☐

DAY 3

At a wax museum you can see life-sized wax figures that are almost

_____ in appearance to famous _____ .

☐
☐

DAY 4

Be careful when you're exploring nature, because some poisonous

_____ look almost _____ to

harmless ones!

☐
☐

DAY 5

A dollhouse is _____ to a real house, except that it's a

_____ version.

☐
☐

TOTAL

unique

DAY 1

REVIEW: identical *adjective*

If you have two notebooks that look _____ on the outside, you

could add _____ to the covers to help you tell them apart.

DAY 2

unique *adjective*

The ability to fly is not _____ to birds in the animal kingdom:

_____ are also able to fly.

DAY 3

I have a _____ relationship with my

_____ , because we can talk to each other about anything.

DAY 4

Something quite _____ about my bedroom is that I have a

_____ .

DAY 5

Being able to _____ is a _____

talent that most people don't have.

TOTAL

SMART START

REVIEW: unique *adjective*

DAY 1

During their dig, archaeologists uncovered some _____ and

valuable artifacts left behind by ancient _____ .

differ *verb*

DAY 2

Our non-fiction reading _____ from our

fiction reading in many ways; for example, when we read non-fiction, we read about

_____ , while when we read fiction, we read stories and poems.

DAY 3

Pineapples _____ greatly from bananas in

_____ .

DAY 4

The country _____ widely from the city; for example,

the country is peaceful and has lots of trees, while the city is busy and has lots of

_____ .

DAY 5

My friend and I like a lot of the same things, but our opinions _____

regarding the movie _____ ;

(he/she) _____ loved it, but I thought it was terrible.

TOTAL

Toolkit Unit 7 | Inference

Inference

To make an **inference**, use a picture or information from text and what we already know to form an idea.

🔍 **Find It**   Look at the picture above. Answer each question and make an **inference**.

What do you already know?	+	What has happened in the picture?	=	My inference
I already know that people are usually happy when their team wins.		Players are _____ because a teammate caught a ball.		I think the team _____ the game.

✏️ **Try It**   Read the headline from the newspaper. Answer each question and make an **inference**.

HEAT WAVE HAS EVERYONE ON ALERT

What do you already know?	+	What does the headline mean?	=	My inference
I already know that a heat wave can be _____.		The headline means that many people are being cautious because of the _____.		So this means I should drink plenty of water, wear light clothing, and avoid the heat by staying _____.

RATE WORD KNOWLEDGE

Rate how well you know Toolkit words you'll use when you make inferences.

3rd Grade	4th Grade	BEFORE	5th Grade	AFTER
decide	conclude	1 2 3 4	**interpret**	1 2 3 4
predict	assume	1 2 3 4	**infer**	1 2 3 4
figure out	conclusion	1 2 3 4	**deduce**	1 2 3 4
probably	assumption	1 2 3 4	**context**	1 2 3 4
clue	determine	1 2 3 4	**presume**	1 2 3 4
prediction	communicate	1 2 3 4	**imply**	1 2 3 4

RATE IT

DISCUSSION GUIDE
- Form groups of four.
- Assign letters to each person.
- Each group member takes a turn leading a discussion.
- Prepare to report about one word.

Ⓐ Ⓑ
Ⓓ Ⓒ

DISCUSS WORDS

Discuss how well you know the fifth grade words. Then, report to the class how you rated each word.

GROUP LEADER **Ask**

So, _____ what do you know
(NAME)

about the word _____ ?

GROUP MEMBERS **Discuss**

1 = I **don't recognize** the word _____ .

   I need to learn what it means.

2 = I **recognize** the word _____ ,

   but I need to learn the meaning.

3 = I'm **familiar** with the word _____ .

   I think it means _____ .

4 = I **know** the word _____ .

   It's a _____ , and it means _____ .
   (PART OF SPEECH)

   Here is my example sentence: _____ .

REPORTER **Report Word Knowledge**

Our group gave the word _____ a rating of _____ because _____ .

SET A GOAL AND REFLECT

First, set a vocabulary goal for this unit by selecting at least three words that you plan to thoroughly learn.
At the end of the unit, return to this page and write a reflection about one word you have mastered.

GOAL

During this unit I plan to thoroughly learn the words _____ ,

_____ , and _____ . Increasing my word knowledge will

help me speak and write effectively when I make an _____ .

As a result of this unit, I feel most confident about the word _____ .

This is my model sentence: _____

_____ .

REFLECTION

interpret
verb

Say it: in • ter • pret

✏️ **Write it:** _____   **Write it again:** _____

🌐 _____

Meaning to understand or explain the meaning of information, actions, or words	**Examples** • My brother said he was fine, but I **interpreted** his body language to mean he was very _____ .
Synonyms • to understand; to explain	• You can often **interpret** the meaning of a _____ by the symbol on it.

Forms
- **Present:**
  I/You/We/They   interpret
  He/She/It   interprets
- **Past:** interpreted

Family
- **Noun:** interpretation

Word Partners
- able/unable to interpret

- interpret the meaning of

Examples
- I wasn't **able to interpret** my mother's gestures to me from across the store, so I walked over to ask her what she wanted.
- Scientists who study ancient cultures have figured out how to **interpret the meaning of** Egyptian hieroglyphs.

✏️ **Try It**

In English class, we often try to **interpret** the meaning of _____ .

VERBAL PRACTICE

Talk about it   Discuss ideas with your partner, listen to classmates, and then write your favorite idea.

Discuss
Listen
Write

1. A mother has to **interpret** the meaning of her baby's cries to understand whether he's _____ or whether he needs a diaper change.

2. I am better able to **interpret** complicated instructions if they include _____ .

interpret
verb

Collaborate

Discuss
Agree
Write
Listen

Discuss ideas with your partner and agree on the best words to complete the frame. ▶

If you _____ how a friend feels based only on her facial expressions

without actually _____ her about how she feels, you can think

everything is fine. Your friend might actually feel _____ .

Our Turn

Discuss
Listen
Write

Read the prompt. Work with the teacher to complete the frames. Write a thoughtful response that includes a relevant example. ▶
PROMPT: Some messages are very short. How can emoticons help the reader interpret the feeling behind the message better?

Emoticons can help you _____ the feeling behind a message by showing

you the writer's _____ . For example, if a writer sends,

"Give me a break!," but includes a picture of a face that's _____ ,

you know that the person is _____ .

Be an Academic Author

Write
Discuss
Listen

Read the prompt and complete the frames. Strengthen your response with a personal experience. ▶
PROMPT: Most packaged foods have a nutrition label. How can interpreting the information on these labels help you when buying a snack?

It's helpful to _____ the information on nutrition labels because

it means you can make _____ choices when buying snacks.

Personally, reading labels helps me avoid foods that have a lot of _____ .

Construct a Response

Write
Discuss
Listen

Read the prompt and construct a thoughtful response. Include a personal experience to strengthen your response.
PROMPT: Describe a time when you said or did something that a friend interpreted the wrong way?

_____

_____

_____

grammar tip ▶

Use the **modal verb**, or helping verb, *can* to show that something is possible. When you use *can*, add a verb in the base form.

EXAMPLE: For our homework tonight, we **can** either write a review of the story we finished in class today, or we **can** write a short story in the voice of the main character. I'm going to write a review.

infer
verb

Say it: in • fer

Write it: _____   Write it again: _____

_____

Meaning
to decide that something is probably true because of what you hear, see, or read

Synonyms
• to figure out

Examples
• When I see people with _____ and cameras, I **infer** that they are tourists.

• During a movie, you can often **infer** from the music when something _____ is about to happen.

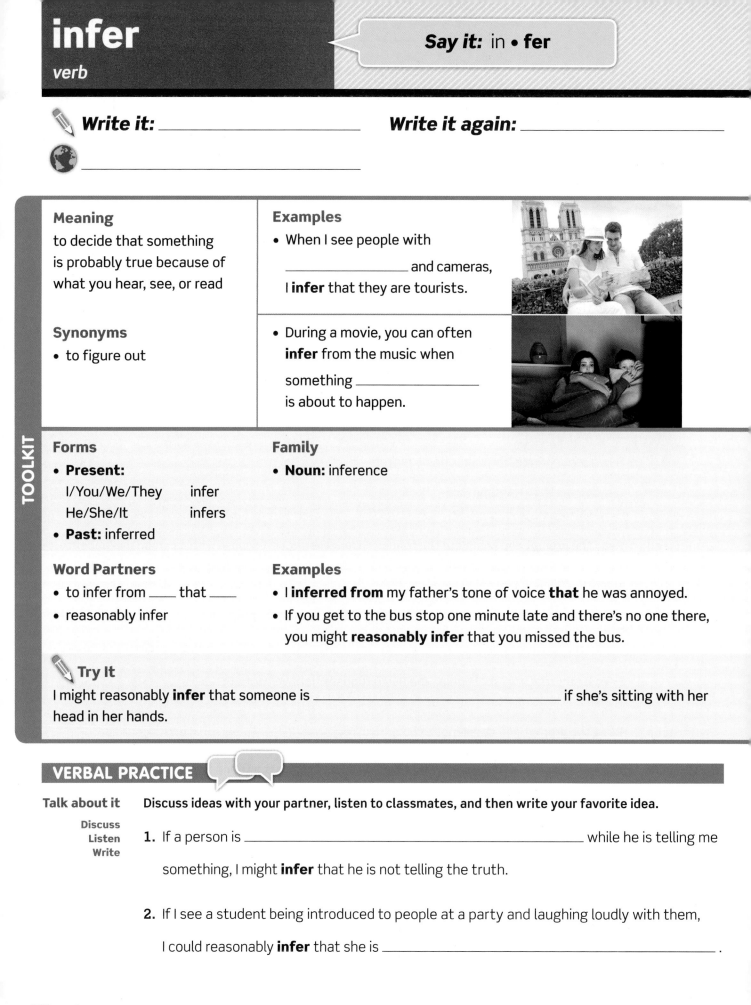

TOOLKIT

Forms
• **Present:**
  I/You/We/They   infer
  He/She/It   infers
• **Past:** inferred

Family
• **Noun:** inference

Word Partners
• to infer from ____ that ____
• reasonably infer

Examples
• I **inferred from** my father's tone of voice **that** he was annoyed.
• If you get to the bus stop one minute late and there's no one there, you might **reasonably infer** that you missed the bus.

Try It
I might reasonably **infer** that someone is _____ if she's sitting with her head in her hands.

VERBAL PRACTICE

Talk about it   Discuss ideas with your partner, listen to classmates, and then write your favorite idea.

Discuss
Listen
Write

1. If a person is _____ while he is telling me something, I might **infer** that he is not telling the truth.

2. If I see a student being introduced to people at a party and laughing loudly with them, I could reasonably **infer** that she is _____ .

WRITING PRACTICE

Collaborate

Discuss
Agree
Write
Listen

Discuss ideas with your partner and agree on the best words to complete the frame. ▶

If the whole class is quiet when the teacher comes into the room, (he/she) _____

might reasonably _____ that we are

_____ .

Our Turn

Discuss
Listen
Write

Read the prompt. Work with the teacher to complete the frames. Write a thoughtful response that includes a convincing reason. ▶

PROMPT: If you saw a book in the library with a dragon on the cover, what might you infer about the book from its cover?

If I saw a library book with a dragon on the cover, I might _____

that it is (a/an) _____ _____ story. I would make

this conclusion because dragons are _____ creatures.

Be an Academic Author

Write
Discuss
Listen

Read the prompt and complete the frames. Strengthen your response with a relevant example.

PROMPT: Animals give signals that tell about their mood. What can we infer from the sounds and movements that animals make?

You can often _____ how an animal feels from the sounds and

movements it makes. For example, if I observe a dog that is _____

_____ , I might reasonably

infer that it feels _____ .

Construct a Response

Write
Discuss
Listen

Read the prompt and construct a thoughtful response. Include a convincing reason to strengthen your response. ▶

PROMPT: A friend suddenly stops answering your text messages and phone calls. What might you infer from this situation and why?

_____

_____

_____

grammar tip ▶

Use the **modal verb**, or helping verb, *might* to show that something is possible. When you use *might*, add a verb in the base form.

EXAMPLE: We **might** have spaghetti for dinner tonight. I hope we do!

deduce
verb

Say it: de • duce

✏️ **Write it:** _____   **Write it again:** _____

🌐 _____

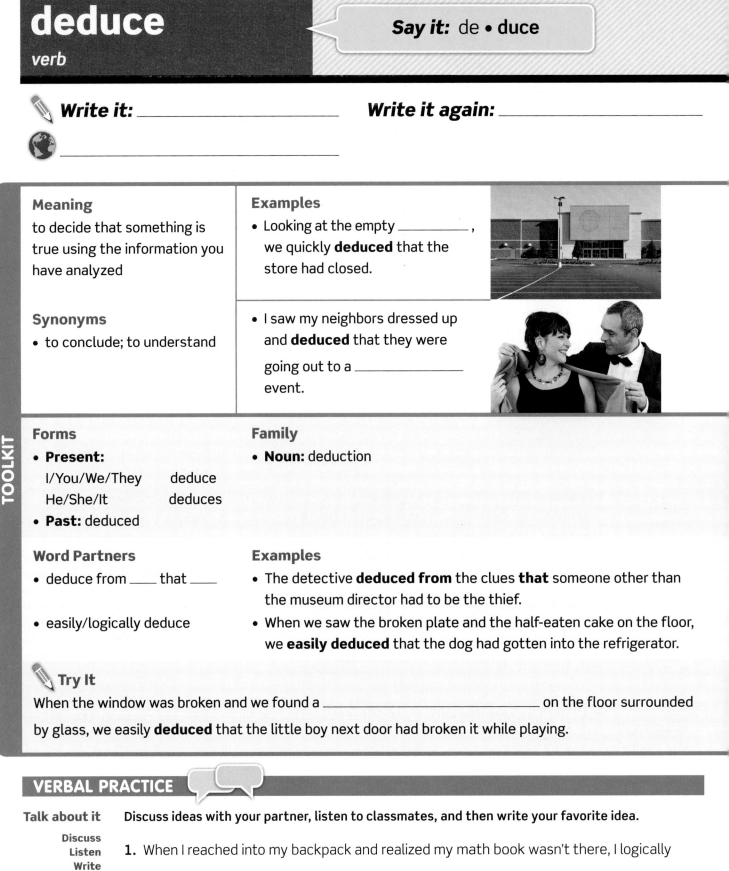

TOOLKIT

Meaning
to decide that something is true using the information you have analyzed

Synonyms
• to conclude; to understand

Examples
• Looking at the empty _____, we quickly **deduced** that the store had closed.

• I saw my neighbors dressed up and **deduced** that they were going out to a _____ event.

Forms
• **Present:**
  I/You/We/They   deduce
  He/She/It   deduces
• **Past:** deduced

Family
• **Noun:** deduction

Word Partners
• deduce from ___ that ___

• easily/logically deduce

Examples
• The detective **deduced from** the clues **that** someone other than the museum director had to be the thief.
• When we saw the broken plate and the half-eaten cake on the floor, we **easily deduced** that the dog had gotten into the refrigerator.

✏️ **Try It**
When the window was broken and we found a _____ on the floor surrounded by glass, we easily **deduced** that the little boy next door had broken it while playing.

VERBAL PRACTICE

Talk about it   Discuss ideas with your partner, listen to classmates, and then write your favorite idea.

Discuss
Listen
Write

1. When I reached into my backpack and realized my math book wasn't there, I logically **deduced** that I had _____ .

2. Before we went into the restaurant, my parents **deduced** from the number of cars in the parking lot that the place would be _____ .

deduce

verb

Collaborate

Discuss
Agree
Write
Listen

Discuss ideas with your partner and agree on the best words to complete the frame. ▶

If the students who bought lunch in the cafeteria ate the food quickly, the rest of us

would _____ that the food was really

_____ that day.

Our Turn

Discuss
Listen
Write

Read the prompt. Work with the teacher to complete the frames. Write a thoughtful response that includes a convincing reason. ▶

PROMPT: Imagine you find your family's garbage can overturned with trash all around it. What would you deduce from this scene?

If I found the garbage can overturned in the morning, I would logically _____

that some _____ had gotten into it. I would think this because these

animals _____ search for scraps in people's trash at night.

Be an Academic Author

Write
Discuss
Listen

Read the prompt and complete the frames. Strengthen your response with a personal experience.

PROMPT: Tests can be hard, but you can deduce an answer on a multiple choice test. How can you do this?

If you're not sure of the correct answer on a multiple choice test, you can _____

it. First eliminate answers that you know are definitely _____ .

Then select the best choice from the remaining options. Personally, I successfully used

this method on _____ tests.

Construct a Response

Write
Discuss
Listen

Read the prompt and construct a thoughtful response. Include a personal experience to strengthen your response.

PROMPT: Describe a time your observations helped you deduce the truth about a situation.

_____

_____

_____

grammar tip ▶

Use the **modal verb**, or helping verb, *would* to show that something is possible under certain conditions. When you use *would*, add a verb in the base form.

EXAMPLE: If I had $50, **I would buy** some new shoes.

context

noun

Say it: con • text

🖉 **Write it:** _____ **Write it again:** _____

🌐 _____

TOOLKIT

Meaning
the situation or events that are connected to someone or something that help you understand it better

Synonyms
• connection

Examples
• Wearing a _____ in the **context** of an office is not surprising, but in a gym, it would look odd.

• Pointing at a person is usually considered rude, but in the **context** of pointing in a _____ , it is not.

Forms
• **Singular:** context
• **Plural:** contexts

Family
• **Adjective:** contextual

Word Partners
• examine the context

• infer from the context that

Examples
• A painting might seem more meaningful if you **examine the context** in which the artist created it.
• If your mother has tears in her eyes and is chopping onions, you can **infer from the context that** her tears are not related to sadness.

🖉 **Try It**
If I see a parent taking a screaming child out of a store, I would infer from the **context** that the child wanted a _____ but didn't get it.

VERBAL PRACTICE

Talk about it Discuss ideas with your partner, listen to classmates, and then write your favorite idea.

Discuss
Listen
Write

1. When I see a photo of an interesting _____ , I try to learn more by examining the **context** of who took it and when it was taken.

2. You don't normally take your shoes off at a restaurant, but in another **context**, such as at a _____ , it would be perfectly acceptable.

WRITING PRACTICE

Collaborate

Discuss
Agree
Write
Listen

Discuss ideas with your partner and agree on the best words to complete the frame. ▶

If you are at a mother-daughter book club, and you see a woman and a girl sitting together

with very different-looking _____ , you might still infer

from the _____ that they are related.

Our Turn

Discuss
Listen
Write

Read the prompt. Work with the teacher to complete the frames. Write a thoughtful response that includes a relevant example to strengthen your response. ▶
PROMPT: In what context might it make sense to see someone walking down the street playing a musical instrument?

It would normally be very unusual to see someone walking down the street playing the

_____ . However, there are _____

in which this might make sense, such as during a _____ .

Be an Academic Author

Write
Discuss
Listen

Read the prompt and complete the frames. Strengthen your response with a relevant example.
PROMPT: When you are reading a story, how might you examine the context of the story? ▶

When I read a story, it's helpful to examine the _____ in which it was written.

For example, I might try to find out as much as I can about the _____

of the story and about the _____ in which the story is set.

Construct a Response

Write
Discuss
Listen

Read the prompt and construct a thoughtful response. Include a relevant example to strengthen your response.
PROMPT: Think of a story you have read that had a historical context. How would examining the context help you to understand the story better?

_____

_____

_____

_____

grammar tip ▶

Use the **modal verb**, or helping verb, *might* to show that something is possible. When you use *might*, add a verb in the base form.

EXAMPLE: I might wear a costume to the party on Friday if I can find a good one.

presume
verb

Say it: pre • sume

✏️ *Write it:* _____ *Write it again:* _____

🌐 _____

TOOLKIT

Meaning
to think that something is probably true, although you are not certain

Synonyms
• to decide; to assume

Examples
• The teacher **presumed** that the _____ children were not paying attention.

• Many people **presume** wrongly that no girls want to become car _____ .

Forms
• **Present:**

| I/You/We/They | presume |
| He/She/It | presumes |

• **Past:** presumed

Family
• **Noun:** presumption

Word Partners
• presume rightly

• presume wrongly

Examples
• I **presumed rightly** that my new neighbors speak Spanish, and it turns out that they are from Puerto Rico.
• Because my brother is very tall, many people **presume wrongly** that he plays basketball, when in fact he plays water polo.

✏️ **Try It**
When I smelled a delicious aroma coming from the kitchen, I **presumed** rightly that my mother was baking

_____ .

VERBAL PRACTICE 💬

Talk about it

Discuss
Listen
Write

Discuss ideas with your partner, listen to classmates, and then write your favorite idea.

1. When a teacher caught a student in the bathroom with a _____

   in his hand, the teacher **presumed** that the student had been writing on the walls.

2. When I saw Janet carrying (a/an) _____ _____

   case to the auditorium, I **presumed** rightly that she was in the orchestra.

WRITING PRACTICE

Collaborate

Discuss
Agree
Write
Listen

Discuss ideas with your partner and agree on the best words to complete the frame. ▶

Before watching the video about ancient Greece, we _____ wrongly

that it would be boring. However, it was actually really _____ !

Our Turn

Discuss
Listen
Write

Read the prompt. Work with the teacher to complete the frames. Write a thoughtful response that includes a relevant example. ▶
PROMPT: **What do some adults sometimes presume wrongly about children your age?**

Sometimes adults _____ wrongly that fifth-graders

are not responsible. However, I am actually quite responsible. For example, I _____

_____ every day.

Be an Academic Author

Write
Discuss
Listen

Read the prompt and complete the frames. Strengthen your response with a convincing reason. ▶
PROMPT: **What do people sometimes presume about you when they first meet you? Do they presume rightly or wrongly?**

People usually _____ that I'm (a/an) _____

_____ person because I often _____ .

Their presumption is actually (right/wrong) _____ , because I really

enjoy _____ .

Construct a Response

Write
Discuss
Listen

Read the prompt and construct a thoughtful response. Include a relevant example to strengthen your response. ▶
PROMPT: **Have you ever presumed something wrongly about someone you didn't know very well? Why did you make that presumption, and how did you learn you were wrong?**

_____

_____

_____

_____

_____

grammar tip ▶

An **adverb** describes an action. Adverbs usually end in *-ly* and come after the verb to describe how the action is done.

EXAMPLE: I always read test questions **carefully** to make sure that I answer them **correctly**.

imply
verb

Say it: im • ply

✎ **Write it:** _____   **Write it again:** _____

🌐 _____

TOOLKIT

Meaning
to suggest that something is true, without saying or showing it directly

Synonyms
• to suggest; to hint at

Examples
• My teacher **implied** that my answer was _____ when he asked me to review it.

• My sister's body language seems to **imply** that she is _____ or bored.

Forms
• **Present:**

| I/You/We/They | imply |
| He/She/It | implies |

• **Past:** implied

Family
• **Noun:** implication
• **Adjective:** Implicit

Word Partners
• seem to imply

• clearly imply

Examples
• My friend's comment that my hair looks "so much better now" since my haircut **seemed to imply** that it didn't look good before.
• When we moved into our new house, the family next door invited us over for dinner, which **clearly implied** that they'd like to be friends.

✎ **Try It**

My friends asked for more of the _____ my mother made, which seemed to **imply** that they really liked it.

VERBAL PRACTICE

Talk about it   Discuss ideas with your partner, listen to classmates, and then write your favorite idea.

Discuss
Listen
Write

1. My friend's _____ expression clearly **implied** that something was wrong.

2. The TV ad for _____ seemed to **imply** that the product is healthy and nutritious, but I doubt that it really is.

WRITING PRACTICE

Collaborate

Discuss
Agree
Write
Listen

Discuss ideas with your partner and agree on the best words to complete the frame. ▶

When a person keeps _____ while

waiting for an appointment, it clearly _____ that she is impatient.

Our Turn

Discuss
Listen
Write

Read the prompt. Work with the teacher to complete the frames. Write a thoughtful response that includes a convincing reason. ▶

PROMPT: Imagine you read a positive article about a city in a magazine. What does the writer's language imply about his or her feelings toward the city?

If I read an article about a city that uses positive adjectives such as _____

_____ and _____ , I would

think that the writer _____ the city. The positive language clearly

_____ this, even if the writer never says it directly.

Be an Academic Author

Write
Discuss
Listen

Read the prompt and complete the frames. Strengthen your response with a convincing reason. ▶

PROMPT: Imagine that a boy comes out of his room in the morning and his mother says: *Are you going to wear that to school?* What does this question seem to imply?

This question seems to _____ that his mother does not

_____ his clothes. If she thought his clothes were

_____ , she would most likely not have asked the question.

Construct a Response

Write
Discuss
Listen

Read the prompt and construct a thoughtful response. Include a convincing reason to strengthen your response. ▶

PROMPT: Do people's clothes clearly imply anything about their personalities?

_____

_____

_____

_____

grammar tip ▶

A **present tense verb** describes an action that happens usually, sometimes, or never. For most verbs that end in *y*, change the *y* to *i* and then add *-es*. For verbs that end in a vowel plus *y*, just add *-s*.

EXAMPLE: A baby kangaroo **stays** in its mother's pouch while she **carries** the baby around.

interpret

REVIEW: differ   *verb*

DAY 1

The clothes you would wear to an expensive restaurant _____

greatly from the clothes you would wear to (a/the) _____

_____ .

☐
☐

interpret   *verb*

DAY 2

If a friend quickly walked by me and didn't say hello, I would _____

that to mean that she was feeling _____ .

☐
☐

DAY 3

The players on a soccer team need to be able to _____ the hand

signals of their _____ .

☐
☐

DAY 4

Some older people are unable to _____ young people's writing

because we use so many abbreviations, like "lol" and " _____ ."

☐
☐

DAY 5

When we do science experiments, first we _____ what

happens, then we _____ the results in a report.

☐
☐

TOTAL

▰◆ SMART START

REVIEW: interpret   *verb*

DAY 1

Many people _____ my grandfather's _____

_____ voice and energetic hand gestures as a sign

that he's upset, but really it's just the way he speaks.

☐
☐

infer   *verb*

DAY 2

If you saw someone on the street who was out of breath, sweating, and wearing shorts

and sneakers, you could reasonably _____ that he had just

_____ .

☐
☐

DAY 3

When someone offers you a mint, you should probably _____

that they are being _____ , and not that you have bad breath!

☐
☐

DAY 4

When I saw my friend's mouth hanging open, I _____ from her

expression that she felt _____ about what I had just told her.

☐
☐

DAY 5

I _____ that my friend didn't like _____

_____ when I noticed that he was picking them

out of his salad.

☐
☐

TOTAL

deduce

REVIEW: infer *verb*

DAY 1

If my friend were sneezing a lot, I would _____ that she had

_____ .

☐

☐

---

deduce *verb*

DAY 2

I _____ from the _____ in my

brother's room that he was sleeping.

☐

☐

DAY 3

If I saw an ambulance racing down the street, I might _____

that there was (a/an) _____ _____ in the neighborhood.

☐

☐

DAY 4

Noticing that my classmate's cheeks were bright red while she gave her presentation,

I _____ that she felt _____

about speaking in front of the class.

☐

☐

DAY 5

If I looked out the window and saw that everyone was wearing _____

_____ , I would logically _____ that it was

warm outside.

☐

☐

TOTAL

▰▰ SMART START

DAY 1

REVIEW: **deduce**   *verb*

When I see dark clouds gathering in the sky, I can _____ that

the weather is going to be _____ .

☐
☐

DAY 2

context   *noun*

People often act differently in different _____ . For example,

someone who is _____ in a group of strangers might be very

confident and outgoing with a group of friends.

☐
☐

DAY 3

To understand what the singer meant when she said that she was tired of writing songs,

you have to read what she said in the _____ of the full

_____ in the magazine.

☐
☐

DAY 4

Laughter is great when you're having fun with your friends, but in a different

_____ , such as a _____ ,

it could be inappropriate.

☐
☐

DAY 5

I met my best friend in the _____ of a

_____ trip for kids from the three elementary schools

in my town.

☐
☐

TOTAL

presume

REVIEW: **context**   *noun*

DAY 1

If I saw a clown at the circus, I would think that was normal, but in another

_____ , such as at (a/the) _____

_____ , I would think it was very weird.

☐

☐

presume   *verb*

DAY 2

I _____ rightly that the _____

were going to be heavy, so I'm glad there was someone there to help me carry them.

☐

☐

DAY 3

When you come across an animal outside, you shouldn't _____

that it's _____ because it could be dangerous.

☐

☐

DAY 4

If I saw one of my classmates limping in the hallway, I would _____

that she had _____ .

☐

☐

DAY 5

When we go to the movies on the weekend, I usually _____

that we will have to wait in line to _____ .

☐

☐

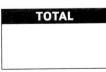

TOTAL

SMART*START*

DAY 1

REVIEW: presume   *verb*

When I saw my mother wearing _____ ,

I _____ that she had been out working in the garden.

☐
☐

DAY 2

imply   *verb*

My friend's comment about the party being "OK" seemed to _____

that she didn't really _____ .

☐
☐

DAY 3

The _____ on my teacher's face when I was talking during

class clearly _____ that she wanted me to stop talking and

pay attention.

☐
☐

DAY 4

When I said I liked your other _____ better, I didn't mean to

_____ that I don't like the one you're wearing now.

☐
☐

DAY 5

In the campaign signs that she hung all over the school, the candidate for class president

_____ that she was _____ than the

other candidates.

☐
☐

TOTAL

Toolkit Unit 8 | Argument

Argument

To make an **argument** means to explain why you believe something is true by supporting it with convincing reasons, relevant examples, and personal experiences.

Find It Read the sentences. Underline the best reason, example, or experience to support each argument.

1. Students should be paid for good grades.

   a. Surveys show that students will work hard if they know they will be rewarded with money.
   b. One reason is that students can buy what they want if they are paid.
   c. For example, good grades show that students understand the lessons.

2. Sodas should be banned from schools.

   a. One reason is that students should have a choice of both sodas and healthy beverages.
   b. For example, some people are allergic to milk.
   c. Research shows that sodas contain a lot of sugar, which can be bad for your health.

Try It Write one convincing reason to support the argument.

Students should not get homework every night. One important reason is that students

_____ .

RATE WORD KNOWLEDGE

Rate how well you know Toolkit words you'll use when you prepare to argue.

3rd Grade	4th Grade	BEFORE	5th Grade	AFTER
discussion	opinion	1 2 3 4	**perspective**	1 2 3 4
believe	fact	1 2 3 4	**persuade**	1 2 3 4
reason	argument	1 2 3 4	**position**	1 2 3 4
agree	convince	1 2 3 4	**reasonable**	1 2 3 4
disagree	evidence	1 2 3 4	**support**	1 2 3 4
experience	convincing	1 2 3 4	**opposing**	1 2 3 4

DISCUSSION GUIDE
- Form groups of four.
- Assign letters to each person. Ⓐ Ⓑ Ⓓ Ⓒ
- Each group member takes a turn leading a discussion.
- Prepare to report about one word.

DISCUSS WORDS

Discuss how well you know the fifth grade words. Then, report to the class how you rated each word.

GROUP LEADER **Ask**

So, _____ what do you know
(NAME)

about the word _____ ?

GROUP MEMBERS **Discuss**

1 = I **don't recognize** the word _____ .

I need to learn what it means.

2 = I **recognize** the word _____ ,

but I need to learn the meaning.

3 = I'm **familiar** with the word _____ .

I think it means _____ .

4 = I **know** the word _____ .

It's a _____ , and it means _____ .
(PART OF SPEECH)

Here is my example sentence: _____ .

REPORTER **Report Word Knowledge**

Our group gave the word _____ a rating of _____ because _____ .

SET A GOAL AND REFLECT

First, set a vocabulary goal for this unit by selecting at least three words that you plan to thoroughly learn. At the end of the unit, return to this page and write a reflection about one word you have mastered.

GOAL

During this unit I plan to thoroughly learn the words _____ ,

_____ , and _____ . Increasing my word knowledge will

help me speak and write effectively when I need to argue a point.

As a result of this unit, I feel most confident about the word _____ .

This is my model sentence: _____

_____ .

REFLECTION

perspective
noun

Say it: per • **spec** • tive

Write it: _____   **Write it again:** _____

_____

TOOLKIT

Meaning
a way of looking at or thinking about something based on your life experiences

Synonyms
• opinion; idea

Examples
• From the toddler's **perspective**, the fountain seems too _____ .

• Children and parents often have different **perspectives** on the importance of wearing _____ .

Forms
• **Singular:** perspective
• **Plural:** perspectives

Word Partners
• from (my, your, his/her, our, their) perspective
• different perspective(s)

Examples
• **From my perspective**, sunny days are better than rainy days because it is more fun to play outside.
• Students and teachers have **different perspectives** on recess. Students want a longer recess, while teachers think it's long enough.

✏️ Try It
From my **perspective**, it is best to do homework after _____

_____ .

VERBAL PRACTICE

Talk about it   Discuss ideas with your partner, listen to classmates, and then write your favorite idea.

Discuss
Listen
Write

1. From my friend's **perspective**, the best TV show is _____

_____ .

2. Parents and children usually have different **perspectives** on _____

_____ .

WRITING PRACTICE

Collaborate

Discuss
Agree
Write
Listen

Discuss ideas with your partner and agree on the best words to complete the frame. ▶

Teachers and students have different _____ on whether

_____ should be permitted during tests.

Our Turn

Discuss
Listen
Write

Read the prompt. Work with the teacher to complete the frames. Write a thoughtful response that includes a convincing reason. ▶
PROMPT: From your perspective, should video games be allowed in schools?

From my _____ , video games (should/should not)

_____ be allowed in schools. One important reason is that

students would _____ .

Be an Academic Author

Write
Discuss
Listen

Read the prompt and complete the frames. Strengthen your response with a relevant example. ▶
PROMPT: What type of music do you and your classmates have different perspectives on?

My classmates and I have different _____

on music. For example, some classmates enjoy _____ ,

but I prefer _____ because it

_____ .

Construct a Response

Write
Discuss
Listen

Read the prompt and construct a thoughtful response. Include a convincing reason to strengthen your response. ▶
PROMPT: Students have different perspectives on the food served in the school cafeteria. Some students prefer more healthy choices, while others want more snack foods. What is your perspective?

_____

_____

_____

grammar tip ▶

Count nouns name things that can be counted. Count nouns have two forms, singular and plural. To make most count nouns plural, add **-s**. When count nouns end in a consonant + *y*, drop the *y* and add *-ies*.

EXAMPLE: My **sisters** and I went to the petting zoo to ride the **ponies**.

persuade
verb

✎ **Write it:** _____   **Write it again:** _____

🌐 _____

Meaning

to convince someone to do or believe something

Synonyms

- convince; encourage

Antonyms

- discourage

Examples

- I tried to persuade my dog to

  take a _____ but he kept jumping out.

- Although he was _____ , I was able to **persuade** my friend to go on the amusement park ride with me.

Forms

- **Present:**

  I/You/We/They   persuade

  He/She/It   persuades

- **Past:** persuaded

Family

- **Noun:** persuasion
- **Adjective:** persuasive
- **Adverb:** persuasively

Word Partners

- try to persuade

- hope to persuade

Examples

- My parents **tried to persuade** me to eat the Brussels sprouts during dinner, but I refused.
- Although I didn't play very well last season, I **hope to persuade** the coach that I'm ready for the team this year.

✎ **Try It**

I hope to **persuade** my friends to _____ with me this weekend.

VERBAL PRACTICE

Talk about it   Discuss ideas with your partner, listen to classmates, and then write your favorite idea.

**Discuss
Listen
Write**

1. It can be difficult to **persuade** a cat to do things, such as to

   _____ .

2. I tried to **persuade** my parents to let me _____

   _____ , but I didn't succeed.

persuade
verb

WRITING PRACTICE

Collaborate

Discuss
Agree
Write
Listen

Discuss ideas with your partner and agree on the best words to complete the frame. ▶

If you hope to _____ someone to help you with (a/an) _____

_____ task, you may have a better chance of success

if you promise to do something for that person in return.

Our Turn

Discuss
Listen
Write

Read the prompt. Work with the teacher to complete the frames. Write a thoughtful response that includes a relevant example. ▶

PROMPT: **How do food companies use advertising to try to persuade us to buy their products?**

Food companies use TV advertisements to try to _____ us that their products

are _____ and delicious. For example, ads for _____

often show children eating the product and looking _____ .

Be an Academic Author

Write
Discuss
Listen

Read the prompt and complete the frames. Strengthen your response with a personal experience. ▶

PROMPT: **When have you persuaded your parents to let you stay up much later than your normal bedtime?**

I recently _____ my parents to let me stay up much later than usual because

I really wanted to _____ .

They agreed because I promised to _____

_____ the next day.

Construct a Response

Write
Discuss
Listen

Read the prompt and construct a thoughtful response. Include a personal experience to strengthen your response. ▶

PROMPT: **Think of a time when someone tried to persuade you to do something you didn't want to do. How did you respond to the person?**

_____

_____

_____

grammar tip ▶

The **preposition** *to* needs to be followed by a base verb.

EXAMPLE: Otters love **to swim** in the water.

position

noun

Say it: po • si • tion

✏️ **Write it:** _____   **Write it again:** _____

🌐 _____

TOOLKIT

Meaning

A person's, organization's, or government's opinion or rule about something

Synonyms

- opinion; rule

Examples

- My personal **position** on keeping animals in _____ is that it is wrong.

- Our school's official **position** on _____ devices is that they are not allowed in the classroom.

Forms

- **Singular:** position
- **Plural:** positions

Word Partners

- official position (on)

- defend (a/my/your/our/ their) position

Examples

- Our teacher's **official position on** eating in class is that we can only take food out during snack time or to celebrate a special occasion.
- In a classroom debate, sometimes you have to **defend a position** you don't actually agree with so you can practice making strong arguments.

✏️ **Try It**

In (a/an) _____ _____ for class, I defended my **position** on the importance of recycling.

VERBAL PRACTICE 💬

Talk about it   Discuss ideas with your partner, listen to classmates, and then write your favorite idea.

Discuss
Listen
Write

1. My parents' official **position** on table manners is that they are essential, so I always have

   to be careful to _____

   _____ .

2. My **position** on space exploration is that it's _____ and so,

   the government (should/should not) _____ continue to fund it.

position

noun

WRITING PRACTICE

Collaborate

Discuss
Agree
Write
Listen

Discuss ideas with your partner and agree on the best words to complete the frame. ▶

Our school's official _____ on bullying is that any student who bullies another

student will be _____ .

Our Turn

Discuss
Listen
Write

Read the prompt. Work with the teacher to complete the frames. Write a thoughtful response that includes a convincing reason. ▶
PROMPT: **What is your personal position on whether girls and boys should play sports together on the same team?**

My personal _____ on this topic is that girls and boys (should/should not)

_____ play on the same team. I believe this because girls and boys have

(different/equal) _____ _____ .

Be an Academic Author

Write
Discuss
Listen

Read the prompt and complete the frames. Strengthen your response with a relevant example. ▶
PROMPT: **What is your position on education? Is it important, and why?**

My _____ on the importance of education is that a good education is

_____ to a good future. For example, you need a good education to get

(a/an) _____ _____ job.

Construct a Response

Write
Discuss
Listen

Read the prompt and construct a thoughtful response. Include a convincing reason to strengthen your response. ▶
PROMPT: **What's your personal position on the topic of school uniforms? Are they a good idea? What is one argument you would use to defend your position?**

_____

_____

_____

_____

grammar tip ▶

An **adjective** describes, or tells about, a noun. Usually an adjective goes before the noun it describes.

EXAMPLE: Vending machines are a **convenient** option for buying snacks at **any** time during the day, but they usually contain **unhealthy** foods and **sugary** drinks.

reasonable
adjective

Say it: rea • so • na • ble

✎ **Write it:** _____   **Write it again:** _____

🌐 _____

TOOLKIT

Meaning
fair and sensible

Synonyms
• understandable

Antonyms
• unreasonable; unfair

Examples
• When I see sale signs in a window, it's **reasonable** to believe that the items are less _____ .

• It's **reasonable** to wear dark _____ outside in the sun, but I don't think it makes sense indoors.

Family
• **Noun:** reason
• **Verb:** reason
• **Adverb:** reasonably

Word Partners
• reasonable argument

• to seem reasonable

Examples
• After our class made some very **reasonable arguments** in favor of having a holiday party, our teacher finally agreed.
• My friend's punishment for talking back to his father **seems reasonable**; he's losing Internet privileges for one week.

✎ **Try It**
Although I've made some **reasonable** arguments for being able to

_____ , my parents will not allow it.

VERBAL PRACTICE

Talk about it   Discuss ideas with your partner, listen to classmates, and then write your favorite idea.

Discuss
Listen
Write

1. It seems **reasonable** to expect every member of a family to

_____ .

2. I think _____ is a **reasonable** amount of time to spend on homework each day.

reasonable

adjective

WRITING PRACTICE

Collaborate

Discuss
Agree
Write
Listen

Discuss ideas with your partner and agree on the best words to complete the frame. ▶

One _____ argument to use with your parents if you want to get a

bike is that you will be able to _____ .

Our Turn

Discuss
Listen
Write

Read the prompt. Work with the teacher to complete the frames. Write a thoughtful response that includes a convincing reason. ▶

PROMPT: Respect for others is important. What do you think is a reasonable consequence for a student who behaves disrespectfully during class?

If a student behaves disrespectfully during class by talking constantly or by being

rude to the teacher, I think a _____ consequence is to

_____ .

I think this would be effective because no one wants to _____

_____ .

Be an Academic Author

Write
Discuss
Listen

Read the prompt and complete the frames. Strengthen your response with a personal experience. ▶

PROMPT: Think about a time you didn't have your homework assignment for class. Did you have a reasonable excuse?

Once, I didn't have my homework assignment for class. I told my teacher it was because the

previous night I had a _____ . My teacher understood

and felt that it was a _____ excuse.

Construct a Response

Write
Discuss
Listen

Read the prompt and construct a thoughtful response. Include a convincing reason to strengthen your response. ▶

PROMPT: Many teachers have a strict policy against chewing gum in the classroom. Does this policy seem reasonable to you? Why or why not?

_____

_____

_____

grammar tip ▶

An **adjective** describes, or tells about, a noun. Usually an adjective goes before the noun it describes.

EXAMPLE: **Natural** peanut butter on **fresh** apple slices makes a **healthy** and **delicious** snack.

support
noun

✏️ **Write it:** _____   **Write it again:** _____

🌐 _____

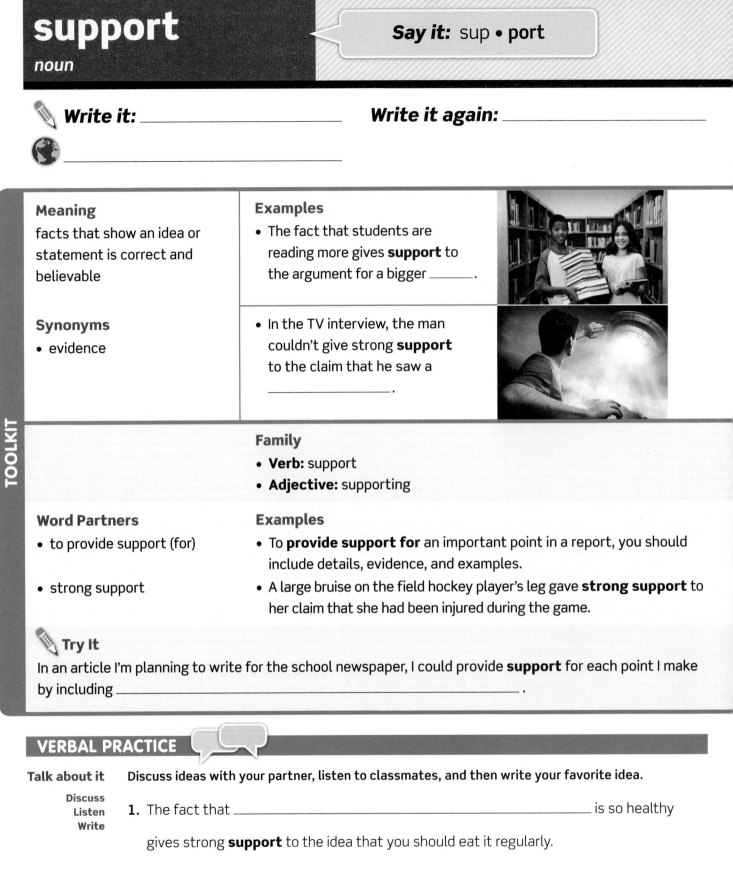

TOOLKIT

Meaning
facts that show an idea or statement is correct and believable

Synonyms
• evidence

Examples
• The fact that students are reading more gives **support** to the argument for a bigger _____.

• In the TV interview, the man couldn't give strong **support** to the claim that he saw a _____.

Family
• **Verb:** support
• **Adjective:** supporting

Word Partners
• to provide support (for)

• strong support

Examples
• To **provide support for** an important point in a report, you should include details, evidence, and examples.
• A large bruise on the field hockey player's leg gave **strong support** to her claim that she had been injured during the game.

✏️ **Try It**
In an article I'm planning to write for the school newspaper, I could provide **support** for each point I make by including _____.

VERBAL PRACTICE 💬

Talk about it   Discuss ideas with your partner, listen to classmates, and then write your favorite idea.

Discuss
Listen
Write

1. The fact that _____ is so healthy gives strong **support** to the idea that you should eat it regularly.

2. Our science book provides **support** for every point it teaches using _____.

WRITING PRACTICE

Collaborate

Discuss
Agree
Write
Listen

Discuss ideas with your partner and agree on the best words to complete the frame. ▶

The students provided strong _____ for their argument to the

principal that their school should have a _____ .

Our Turn

Discuss
Listen
Write

Read the prompt. Work with the teacher to complete the frames. Write a thoughtful response that includes a personal experience. ▶

PROMPT: Think of a time you convinced your parents to let you do something. What arguments did you make in support of your request?

Once, I convinced my parents to let me _____ .

To provide _____ for my argument, I pointed out that I'm

trustworthy and mature, so they could depend on me to _____

_____ .

Be an Academic Author

Write
Discuss
Listen

Read the prompt and complete the frames. Strengthen your response with a relevant example. ▶

PROMPT: Think of a topic you would like to present to your class. What visual aid could you use to provide support for this topic during a presentation?

During a presentation, I could use a visual aid to provide _____ for my

topic. For example, if my topic was _____ ,

I could use a _____

_____ to help my classmates understand the topic better.

Construct a Response

Write
Discuss
Listen

Read the prompt and construct a thoughtful response. Include a personal experience to strengthen your response. ▶

PROMPT: Think of a time when someone didn't believe something you said. How did you provide support for your claim to prove that it was factual?

_____

_____

_____

grammar tip ▶

Noncount nouns name things that cannot be counted in English. Noncount nouns have the same form for "one" or "more than one." Do not add **-s** to a noncount noun to make it plural.

EXAMPLE: She has a lot of **experience** making different flavors of homemade **ice cream**.

opposing

adjective

Say it: op • po • sing

✎ **Write it:** _____   **Write it again:** _____

🌐 _____

Meaning

completely different from another idea or opinion

Synonyms
• different

Antonyms
• similar

Examples
• Siblings often have **opposing** opinions about what _____ to watch on television.

• In a debate, one student presents arguments on a _____ , and another student presents **opposing** arguments.

Family
• **Noun:** opposition
• **Verb:** oppose
• **Adjective:** opposite

Word Partners

• opposing opinions (about)

• opposing views (on)

Examples
• My mother and father have **opposing opinions about** how much I should study during the weekend.
• My uncle and aunt have **opposing views on** pet ownership. He thinks pets are great, but she thinks they are messy and too much work.

✎ **Try It**

Adults and children often have **opposing** views on which _____ are the most interesting.

VERBAL PRACTICE

Talk about it

**Discuss
Listen
Write**

Discuss ideas with your partner, listen to classmates, and then write your favorite idea.

1. My best friend and I have **opposing** opinions about the game _____

_____ . I don't think it's fun at all, but (he/she) _____

loves it.

2. An argument for playing football is that it is _____ .

An **opposing** argument is that playing football can be dangerous.

opposing
adjective

WRITING PRACTICE

Collaborate

Discuss
Agree
Write
Listen

Discuss ideas with your partner and agree on the best words to complete the frames. ▶

Some teachers and students have _____ views on the school dress

code. Some students feel they should be able to wear _____ to

school, while some teachers think that would be inappropriate.

Our Turn

Discuss
Listen
Write

Read the prompt. Work with the teacher to complete the frames. Write a thoughtful response that includes a convincing reason. ▶

PROMPT: **What opposing views do adults and children your age have about cell phone privacy?**

Adults and children often have _____ views about cell

phone privacy. For example, many children think that they should be able to

_____ at any time. However, parents often want

to know about every _____ on the cell phone.

Be an Academic Author

Write
Discuss
Listen

Read the prompt and complete the frames. Strengthen your response with a personal experience. ▶

PROMPT: **When arguing an opposing view, what is an effective way to defend your position?**

When arguing, one effective way to defend your position is to learn more about the

_____ view. Then, gather _____ to

demonstrate that your view is more _____ .

Construct a Response

Write
Discuss
Listen

Read the prompt and construct a thoughtful response. Include a convincing reason to strengthen your response. ▶

PROMPT: **Some people think that the school year should be longer. What is one opposing argument?**

_____

_____

_____

grammar tip ▶

Adjectives are always singular even if they describe a plural noun. Do not add **-s** to adjectives that describe plural nouns.

EXAMPLE: There are **red** grapes and **green** apples in the fruit bowl.

perspective

⚑⚑ SMART START

REVIEW: imply *verb*

DAY 1

When I told my friend I had to cancel our plans, her tone of voice

_____ that she was _____ .

perspective *noun*

DAY 2

From my _____ , it's really hard to learn how to

_____ .

DAY 3

If you and your friend have different _____

on an important issue, you should always try to discuss your ideas in a

_____ manner and not get into an argument.

DAY 4

My mother and I have different _____ on whether or not

it's really necessary for me to _____ every day.

DAY 5

From my _____ , the most fun indoor game to play is

_____

TOTAL

⚑ SMART*START*

DAY 1

REVIEW: perspective *noun*

From my _____ , _____

is more interesting and fun than sitting around watching TV.

persuade *verb*

DAY 2

You could never _____ my little brother to eat

_____ under any circumstances.

DAY 3

I hope to _____ my parents to have

my birthday party at (a/an) _____

_____ , because I think it would be fun.

DAY 4

My classmates and I tried to _____ our teacher to give us

more time on our _____ .

DAY 5

One activity you could easily _____ me to do every day is

_____ .

TOTAL

position

DAY 1

REVIEW: persuade *verb*

I wanted to stay on the couch and watch TV, but instead my friend

_____ me to

_____ outside.

position *noun*

DAY 2

My _____ on the subject of video games is that kids

(should/shouldn't) _____ play them because many video

games are quite _____ .

DAY 3

My parents' official _____ on chores is that if I don't

complete them, then I won't be able to _____ .

DAY 4

My _____ regarding physical education at school is that

it's (as/not as) _____ _____ as

academic subjects like math, science, and English.

DAY 5

Our teacher's official _____ on homework is that it must

never be _____ .

TOTAL

⚐▶▰ SMART START

DAY 1

My _____ on the topic of artificial sweeteners is that people ☐

are better off using natural sweeteners like _____ . ☐

---

reasonable *adjective*

DAY 2

One _____ argument in favor of getting a pet is that a pet ☐

_____ . ☐

DAY 3

I think that one hour is a _____ amount of time to spend

_____ every day. ☐

☐

DAY 4

It seems _____ to expect people who live near the

_____ to walk there instead of driving or taking the bus.

☐

☐

DAY 5

If you have a close friend, it's _____ to expect

him or her to offer you _____ when you need it, ☐

without asking for anything in return. ☐

TOTAL

support

REVIEW: reasonable *adjective*

DAY 1

Once children reach the age of ten, I think it's _____ for their

parents to let them _____ by themselves.

support *noun*

DAY 2

If you want people to agree with an unpopular _____ , you'll

really need to provide strong _____ for your arguments.

DAY 3

In _____ of my claim that

_____ is a great movie,

I would just ask you to watch it with me so you could see for yourself.

DAY 4

She gave _____ to her claim that she was a creative person

by _____ right on the spot.

DAY 5

You could find scientific research on the Internet to provide _____

for the argument that _____

(is/are) _____ harmful to our health.

TOTAL

⚐ SMART START

REVIEW: support *noun*

DAY 1

Three witnesses provided _____ for the student's claim ☐

that another student had _____ him in the hallway. ☐

opposing *adjective*

DAY 2

An argument in favor of homework is that it helps students reinforce what they learn in

class, but an _____ argument might be that children should ☐

spend their afternoons _____ . ☐

DAY 3

My friend and I have _____ opinions on who is the best

☐

_____ . ☐

DAY 4

Some children my age have _____ views about

_____ . Some think they're only for younger children, while ☐

others still enjoy them. ☐

DAY 5

If you and your best friend have _____ opinions

about what to do after school, you should talk about it and try to find (a/an)

_____ _____ that makes ☐

you both happy. ☐

TOTAL

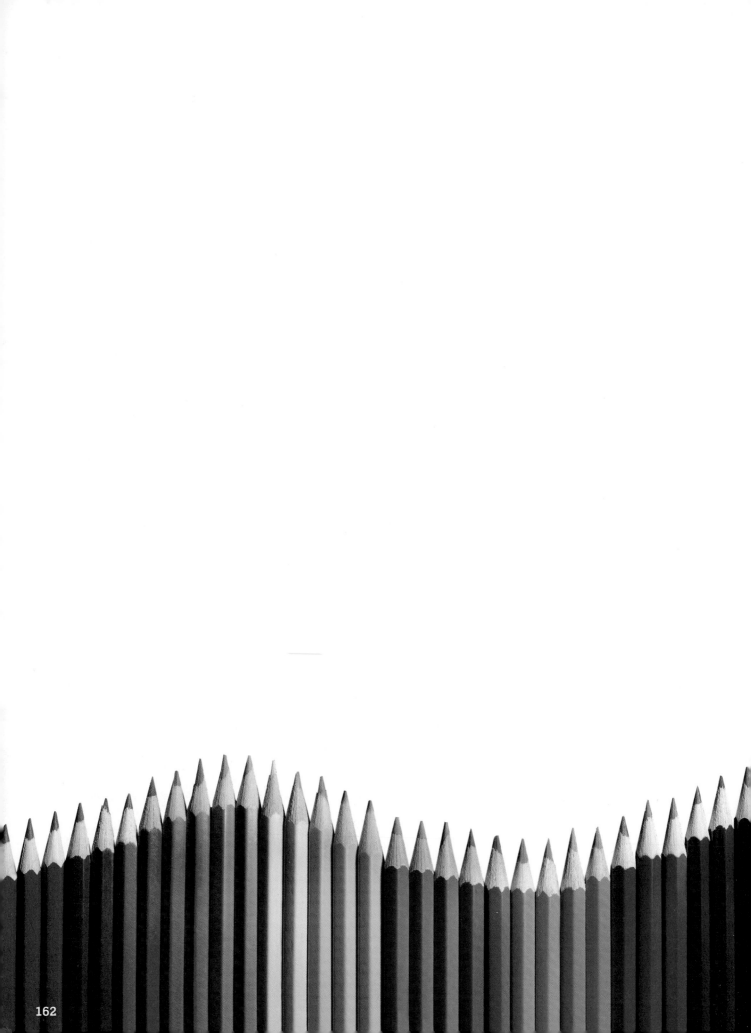

▶ grammar lessons

grammar

▶ **Present Tense Verbs**

Use the **present tense** when you talk about actions that happen usually, sometimes, or regularly.

	Subject	Verb
Use the **base form** of the verb when the subject is *I, you, we,* or *they.*	I You We They	**read** the book. base form
Use the **-s** form of the verb when the subject is *he, she,* or *it.*	He She It	**reads** the book. -s form

- When the base form of the verb ends in *s, sh, ch,* or *x,* add **-es:**
  miss ➞ *misses; wash* ➞ *washes; catch* ➞ *catches; fix* ➞ *fixes*
- When the base form of the verb ends in a consonant + *y,* change the *y* to *i* and add **-es:** *cry* ➞ *cries*

Find It

Read the sentences. Write the correct form of the present tense verb.

1. On Tuesdays, Lucy (stay/stays) _____ late after school to participate in the drama club.

2. Dolphins (use/uses) _____ a blowhole on top of their heads to breathe.

3. My mother, sister, and I usually (cook/cooks) _____ a large pancake breakfast on Sunday mornings.

4. The longest river in the world, the Nile, (flow/flows) _____ 4,200 miles from Uganda through Sudan and Egypt.

Try It

Complete the sentences using the correct form of the verb.

1. Camouflage (protect) _____ animals from being attacked by other animals.

2. Whenever we have a 5th grade class event, I (take) _____ photos for the yearbook.

3. Your blood (carry) _____ oxygen to all parts of your body.

4. Every day my brother (hurry) _____ to the bus and usually just makes it at the last minute.

Discuss and Write

Collaborate Work with a partner. Use the correct form of the verbs to complete the sentences.

Discuss
Agree
Write
Listen

1. rise/set   The sun _____ in the east and

_____ in the west.

2. cause/
come   Cutting onions releases a gas which _____ a

stinging sensation when the gas _____ into

contact with your eyes.

3. hold/
dance   Every year, the city of Rio de Janeiro in Brazil

_____ a fantastic carnival during which

people _____ through the streets in colorful

costumes.

4. worry/
relax   My best friend _____ too much about all sorts

of things and hardly ever _____ .

Your Turn Work independently. Use the correct form of the verbs and your own words to complete the

Think
Write   sentences.

1. itch/run   During allergy season she is _____

because her eyes _____ and her nose

_____ .

2. ask/give   My friends often _____ for my

advice because they know I _____

_____ advice.

3. avoid/stick   Jonah _____ foods

like _____ because it

_____ to his braces.

grammar

▶ **Adjectives and Adverbs**

An **adjective** describes a noun.

An **adverb** describes a verb.

Adjective	Adverb
She is a **creative** student.	She writes **creatively**.
We have an **enthusiastic** class.	We do our work **enthusiastically**.
My older brother is a **punctual** person.	He always arrives **punctually**.

- An adjective usually comes before the noun it describes. An adjective can also come directly after the verb *be*: New York City is big.
- An adverb usually comes after the verb it describes. Most adverbs are formed by adding **-ly** to an adjective: *careful* ➝ *carefully*

Find It

Complete the sentences with either the adjective or the adverb.

1. She spoke (cheerful/cheerfully) _____ about her upcoming birthday.

2. The (foolish/foolishly) _____ criminal left behind so many clues, it was easy for the police to catch him.

3. My little sister ate up the bag of popcorn (greedy/greedily) _____ .

4. I am not the most (graceful/gracefully) _____ person. I trip all of the time!

Try It

Complete the sentences using the correct form (adjective or adverb) of the word.

1. Mr. Gonzales is a (kind) _____ teacher who takes a real interest in his students.

2. My aunt teases my uncle about his voice because he sings (terrible) _____ .

3. We put the nest back in the tree (careful) _____ to avoid disturbing the eggs.

4. Alex is a (dependable) _____ person who always finishes any task he is given.

Discuss and Write

Collaborate Work with a partner. Write the sentence, including the adverb or adjective provided.

Discuss
Agree **1.** (impressive)   You gave a presentation.
Write
Listen
_____

_____ .

2. (promptly)   He arrived for his appointment.

_____

_____ .

3. (proudly)   The parents watched as their daughter graduated.

_____

_____ .

Your Turn Work independently. Use the correct form of the word (adjective or adverb) and your own words
Think   to complete the sentences.
Write

1. (polite)   The shopkeeper spoke _____ to the

_____ customer.

2. (interesting)   I think _____ is

one of the most _____ books I have ever read.

3. (serious)   We had a _____ conversation about the dangers of

_____ .

4. (passionate)   The environmentalist who visited our class spoke _____

about the importance of _____ the

environment.

grammar

▶ **Adverbs of Frequency**

Use **adverbs of frequency** to talk about how often actions happen.

Adverbs of Frequency		Examples with the Verb *Be*	Examples with Other Verbs
100%	always	I **am always** with my grandfather on Saturday afternoon.	I **always visit** my grandfather on Saturday afternoon.
	usually	She **is usually** energetic.	She **usually has** a lot of energy.
	often	We **are often** hungry after school.	We **often have** a snack after school.
	sometimes	They **are sometimes** late to school.	They **sometimes miss** the bus.
	rarely	My little brother **is rarely** rude.	My little brother **rarely speaks** rudely.
0%	never	My dog **is never** calm.	My dog **never sits** calmly.

- Put adverbs of frequency after the verb *be*.
- Put adverbs of frequency before all other verbs.

🔍 Find It

Read the pairs of sentences. Underline the sentence that has the adverb of frequency in the right place.

1. It always seems to rain on Monday. | It seems always to rain on Monday.

2. I often misspell the word *separate*. | I misspell often the word *separate*.

3. We have sometimes parties in class. | We sometimes have parties in class.

4. She is rarely allowed to stay up past 10:00 on weekdays. | She rarely is allowed to stay up past 10:00 on weekdays.

✏️ Try It

Write the sentence and include the adverb of frequency. Be sure to put it in the correct place.

1. (always) Tulips are the first flower to bloom in our school garden each spring.

_____

2. (rarely) It is very cold in India.

_____

3. (usually) I borrow two or three books from the library each week.

_____

Discuss and Write

Collaborate

Discuss
Agree
Write
Listen

Work with a partner. Complete the sentences using appropriate adverbs of frequency and your own words.

1. He _____ chooses novels because he prefers to read

_____ instead of made-up stories.

2. Sarah _____ eats meats like hot dogs and

_____ because she's a vegetarian.

3. My computer _____ crashes when I have too many

_____ open.

4. On Fridays, for a treat, we _____ buy

_____ on our way home from school.

Your Turn

Think
Write

Work independently. Complete the sentences using appropriate adverbs of frequency and your own words.

1. I _____ walk to school, but it is so

_____ outside today that I took the bus.

2. My mother _____ wears sweatshirts because she thinks

they look _____ .

3. David is _____ friendly and _____

which is why people like him so much.

4. I _____ eat _____ , but every

once in a while I get a craving for (it/them) _____ and eat a lot.

grammar

▶ **Present Progressive Tense**

Use the **present progressive** to talk about an action that is happening right now.

Subject	be	Verb + *ing*
I	am	
He She It	is	download**ing** a new book.
You We They	are	

- To form the progressive tense of most verbs, add **-ing** to the base form of the verb: read ⟶ *reading*
- For verbs that end in a consonant + **-e**, drop the **-e** before adding **-ing**: dance ⟶ *dancing*

Find It

Complete the sentences using the correct form of the verb.

1. The water is (boil) _____ , so I'll put the pasta in now.

2. My favorite author is (write) _____ a sequel to my favorite book!

3. The stars are (shine) _____ brightly in the sky tonight.

Try It

Read the present tense sentences. Write the sentences as present progressive sentences.

1. The squirrels eat the seeds and nuts in the birdfeeder.

   _____

2. I work my way through my list of chores.

   _____

3. The volcano erupts.

   _____

grammar

Discuss and Write

Collaborate

Discuss
Agree
Write
Listen

Work with a partner. Use the correct form of the verbs to complete the sentences.

1. watch/
   cheer

   We're _____ the baseball game and

   _____ for our team.

2. compare/
   contrast

   We are _____ and _____

   the characters in the short story we just read.

3. try/talk

   I'm _____ to listen to the dialogue in the movie,

   but too many people in the audience are _____ .

Your Turn

Think
Write

Work independently. Use the correct form of the verbs and your own words to complete the
sentences.

1. annoy/
   throw

   My baby brother is _____ me by

   _____ little pieces of _____

   at me.

2. organize/
   arrange

   I'm _____ the bookshelf by

   _____ the books in order according to

   _____ .

3. sort/glue

   The preschoolers are _____ shapes, then

   _____ all of the circles to a

   _____ .

4. bake/
   prepare

   My aunts are _____ a chocolate cake and

   _____ orange sauce right now. The smells are

   _____ .

grammar
▶ Past Tense Verbs

Use the **past tense** to talk about events or actions that have already happened.

Subject	Base Form of Verb + -ed/-d	
I He She It You We They	watch**ed**	a new program last night.

- To form the simple past tense of most regular verbs, add **-ed** to the base form of the verb: *listen* ⟶ *listened*
- For regular verbs that end in **-e**, add **-d**: *smile* ⟶ *smiled*

🔍 Find It

Read the sentences. Write the correct form of the verb.

1. We (learn/learned) _____ about the water cycle in third grade.

2. My family and I (like/liked) _____ programs about nature and wildlife.

3. During the Middle Ages, people (believe/believed) _____ that the earth was flat.

4. I (attend/attended) _____ a karate class after school every Wednesday.

✏️ Try It

Complete the sentences using the correct form of the verb.

1. Prehistoric artists (paint) _____ pictures of people and animals on cave walls.

2. I was going to audition for the school play, but then I (change) _____ my mind.

3. Alexander Graham Bell (invent) _____ the telephone in 1876.

4. I think the second draft of my paper is much better than the first because I (revise) _____ it carefully.

Discuss and Write

Collaborate Work with a partner. Use the correct form of the verbs to complete the sentences.

Discuss
Agree
Write
Listen

1. applaud/
bow

After the play, the audience _____ while the

actors _____ .

2. kick/score

During last week's game, Sophie _____ the ball

and _____ a point for her team.

3. watch/
land

In 1969, people all around the world _____ on

television as astronauts _____ on the moon

for the first time.

Your Turn Work independently. Use the correct form of the verbs and your own words to complete the

Think
Write

sentences.

1. clean/spill

Right after we _____ the

kitchen, my baby sister _____

_____ all over the floor.

2. download/
show

My older brother _____ (a/an) _____

_____ math app on his tablet yesterday and

_____ me how to use it.

3. sprain/
scrape

Sebastian _____ his ankle and

_____ his knee while he was

_____ yesterday.

4. misplace/
look

Yesterday, I _____ my keys and

_____ all over for them, then finally

found them (in/on) _____ the

_____ .

grammar

▶ **Possessive Nouns**

Use **possessive nouns** to show that something belongs to someone or something.

	Singular Noun	Possessive Noun	Example
To show that something belongs to someone or something, add an apostrophe (') and -s at the end of a singular noun.	book	book's	The book's cover is beautiful.

	Plural Noun that ends in -s	Possessive Noun	Example
To show that something belongs to more than one person or thing, add an apostrophe (') at the end of a plural noun, following the –s.	books	books'	The books' covers are beautiful.

🔍 Find It

Complete the sentences using the correct possessive noun.

1. The (newspaper's/newspapers') _____ headline was surprising.

2. The (earth's/earths') _____ gravity stops us from floating off into space.

3. Both (actor's / actors') _____ names begin with the letter J.

4. This (book's /books') _____ pages are yellow with age.

✏️ Try It

Complete the sentences with the correct possessive form of the noun.

1. Thomas Jefferson was (America) _____ third president.

2. (Monkeys) _____ hands have thumbs.

3. All five (boys) _____ uniforms are maroon and white.

4. You should cut the (candle) _____ wick shorter before you light it.

Discuss and Write

Collaborate

Discuss
Agree
Write
Listen

Work with a partner. Read the first sentence. Then complete the second sentence with the correct possessive noun.

1. The frame of the picture is too small.

   The _____ frame is too small.

2. The roots of the plant absorb water from the soil.

   The _____ roots absorb water from the soil.

3. The rooftops of those buildings have gardens.

   Those _____ rooftops have gardens.

4. The mayor listened to the complaints of the protesters.

   The mayor listened to the _____ complaints.

Your Turn

Think
Write

Work independently. Complete the sentences with the correct possessive form of the noun and your own words.

1. (dressers)   There are three dressers in my room, and the

   _____ drawers are stuffed with

   _____ .

2. (cellphones)   All the _____ rings sound different.

   For example, some sound like a dog barking and some sound like a

   _____ .

3. (mother)   My _____ perfume reminds me of

   _____ .

4. (wizard)   In the story I read to my little sister, the _____

   hat is full of _____ .

grammar

▶ **There, Their, They're**

There, **their**, and **they're** are homophones. Homophones are words that have the same sound but are spelled differently and have different meanings.

Word	Explanation	Example
there	*There* is an adverb that means *that place.* *There* is also used with the verb *be* to introduce a sentence or clause.	The non-fiction section is over **there**. **There** are two desserts to choose from.
their	*Their* shows ownership. It is always followed by a noun.	The tourists took out **their** cameras.
they're	*They're* is a contraction formed by putting together the words *they + are.*	**They're** working on the project together.

Find It

Read the sentences. Choose the correct word to complete the sentences.

1. You must take these books back to the library. (Their/They're) _____

   overdue.

2. Scientists do experiments to test (their/they're) _____ theories.

3. The frozen yogurt shop gets crowded on Friday night. I don't really want to go (their/there)

   _____ tonight.

4. Fish use (there/their) _____ gills to breathe underwater.

Try It

Complete the sentences using *there*, *their*, or *they're*.

1. Jana and Estella are going to middle school next year. _____ very excited

   about starting a new school.

2. _____ are about one billion people in the world who speak Mandarin Chinese.

3. The children walked through poison ivy, and now _____ legs are covered in an

   itchy rash.

grammar

▶ **There, Their, They're**

Discuss and Write

Collaborate

Discuss
Agree
Write
Listen

Work with a partner. Complete the sentences using *there, their,* and *they're.*

1. I don't think Ana and Felix are home. I keep calling _____ house, but _____ not answering _____ phone.

2. We used to eat pizza _____ all of the time, but they changed _____ recipe and we don't like it as much anymore.

3. _____ are reference books in our library which we can't check out. _____ only to be used in the library.

Your Turn

Think
Write

Work independently. Complete the sentences with *there, their,* and *they're* and your own words.

1. The Wu family is growing _____ own vegetables this summer. _____ growing broccoli, _____ and _____ .

2. _____ upset because _____ are scratches on _____ new _____ .

3. Cora and Kayla are twins. _____ so alike that even _____ _____ sometimes have trouble telling them apart.

4. The new parents dressed _____ babies up as _____ for _____ first Halloween.

grammar

▶ **Modal Verbs**

A **modal verb** is a helping verb that adds more meaning to the main verb.

Example Sentences	Subject	Modal	Base Form of Verb		Meaning
Our soccer team **could** win the championship.	Our soccer team	**could**	win	the championship.	Use *could* to show that something might be possible.
We **should** eat less sugar.	We	**should**	eat	less sugar.	Use *should* to make suggestions or recommendations.
She **would** take guitar lessons if she had a guitar.	She	**would**	take	guitar lessons if she had a guitar.	Use *would* to show that something is possible under certain conditions.

Find It

Read the sentences. Complete the sentences with the best modal choice.

1. We (would/could) _____ plan a party for Ella's birthday, or just take her

   out to dinner and a movie.

2. She hurt your feelings. You (should/would) _____ tell her.

3. If some types of sharks stopped moving, they (should/would) _____ die.

4. Liam (would/should) _____ play soccer, but he sprained his ankle yesterday.

Try It

Complete the sentences with the correct modal + verb forms.

1. You (should are/should be) _____ careful not to post personal

   information on the internet.

2. The giant tortoise has the longest life of any animal and (could lives/could live)

   _____ 100 years or more.

3. Our dog (would eats/would eat) _____ the whole bag of dog food if we

   let him!

Discuss and Write

Collaborate

Discuss
Agree
Write
Listen

Work with a partner. Complete the sentences with the best modal choices. Use the modals *could*, *should*, and *would*.

1. Tigers _____ become extinct soon. We

   _____ do more to protect these beautiful animals.

2. I bet Meera _____ watch your hamster for you while you

   and your family are away if you _____ leave the hamster

   and some hamster food with her.

3. My room is a mess. I really _____ clean it, but it

   _____ probably take the entire day.

4. I _____ either go to an amusement park with

   my family tomorrow or go to my friend's birthday party. What do you think I

   _____ do?

Your Turn

Think
Write

Work independently. Choose the best modal and your own words to complete the sentences. Use the modals *could*, *should*, and *would*.

1. My parents said they _____ let me get my ears pierced if

   I promise to _____ .

2. People _____ try to recycle things like paper towel rolls and

   _____ instead of throwing them away.

3. If you're having trouble understanding the _____ ,

   I _____ try to help you with it.

4. _____ is one of the best books I've ever

   read. I really think you _____ read it.

Acknowledgments, continued from page ii

vi (tl) ©Aspen Photo/Shutterstock.com, (cr) ©sashahaltam/Shutterstock.com, (cl) ©gengirl/Shutterstock.com.com, (b) ©Juriah Mosin/Shutterstock.com. **viii** (tl) ©Darrin Henry/Shutterstock.com, (cr) ©Santhosh Varghese/Shutterstock.com, (cl) ©Robert Harding Picture Library Ltd/Alamy, (b) ©Kreangkrai Indarodom/Shutterstock.com. **x** (tl) ©Tyler Olson/Shutterstock.com, (cr) ©Alan Bailey/Shutterstock.com, (cl) ©Getty Images, (b) ©Marmaduke St. John/Alamy. **2** ©Zurijeta/Shutterstock.com. **4** (t) ©karelnoppe/Shutterstock.com, (b) ©cbpix/Shutterstock.com. **6** (t) ©Stefano Tinti/Shutterstock.com, (b) ©Alon Othnay/Shutterstock.com. **8** (t) ©bikeriderlondon/Shutterstock.com, (b) ©Monkey Business Images/Shutterstock.com. **10** (t) ©Nataliya Kuznetsova/Shutterstock.com, (b) ©prudkov/Shutterstock.com. **12** (t) ©snapgalleria/Shutterstock.com, (b) ©Concept Photo/Shutterstock.com. **14** (t) ©Jeroen van den Broek/Shutterstock.com, (b) ©Jaimie Duplass/Shutterstock.com. **22** ©Baloncici/Shutterstock.com. **24** (t) ©Igor Borodin/Shutterstock.com, (b) ©Poznyakov/Shutterstock.com. **26** (t) ©Blend Images/Shutterstock.com, (b) ©Dan Moeller/Shutterstock.com. **28** (t) ©Holly Harris/The Image Bank/Getty Images, (b) ©Juice Images/Alamy. **30** (t) ©newcorner/Shutterstock.com, (b) ©Mega Pixel/Shutterstock.com. **32** (t) ©Yellow Dog Productions/Digital Vision/Getty Images, (b) ©Monkey Business Images/Shutterstock.com. **34** (t) ©Viacheslav Nikolaenko/Shutterstock.com, (b) ©tci/MARKA/Alamy. **42** ©JGI/Jamie Grill/Blend Images/Getty Images. **44** (t) ©sashahaltam/Shutterstock.com, (b) ©YuryZap/Shutterstock.com. **46** (t) ©Blend Images/Shutterstock.com, (b) ©Morgan Lane Photography/Shutterstock.com. **48** (t) ©Jeroen van den Broek/Shutterstock.com, (b) ©Peter Elvidge/Shutterstock.com. **50** (t) ©Stacy Barnett/Shutterstock.com, (b) ©Erik Svoboda/Shutterstock.com. **52** (t) ©Ysbrand Cosijn/Shutterstock.com, (b) ©Jill Chen/Shutterstock.com. **54** (t) ©Aspen Photo/Shutterstock.com, (b) ©pixshots/Shutterstock.com. **62** ©Oxford Scientific/Getty Images. **64** (t) ©gengirl/Shutterstock.com, (b) ©Shutterstock.com. **66** (t) ©Anton_Ivanov/Shutterstock.com, (b) ©Image Source/Alamy. **68** (t) ©Yaping/Shutterstock.com, (b) ©Denis Kuvaev/Shutterstock.com. **70** (t) ©Andrew Rubtsov/Alamy, (b) ©Sally Scott/Shutterstock.com. **72** (t) ©cristi180884/Shutterstock.com, (b) ©Juriah Mosin/Shutterstock.com. **74** (t) ©Pete Niesen/Shutterstock.com, (b) ©photka/Shutterstock.com. **82** ©Monkey Business Images/Shutterstock.com. **84** (t) ©Santhosh Varghese/Shutterstock.com, (b) ©Heiko Kiera/Shutterstock.com, (b) ©Darrin Henry/Shutterstock.com, (b) ©WDG Photo/Shutterstock.com. **88** (t) ©Christopher Tan Teck Hean/Shutterstock.com, (b) ©Martin Valigursky/Shutterstock.com. **90** (t) ©Fotokostic/Shutterstock.com, (b) ©Dudarev Mikhail/Shutterstock.com. **92** (t) ©Suzanne Long/Alamy, (b) ©YK/Shutterstock.com. **94** (t) ©Karen Struthers/Shutterstock.com, (b) ©Amy Myers/Shutterstock.com. **102** ©rvlsoft/Shutterstock.com. **104** (t) ©KidStock/Getty Images, (b) ©Elena Elisseeva/Shutterstock.com. **106** (t) ©Jan-Dirk Hansen/Shutterstock.com, (b) ©Joana Kruse/Alamy. **108** (t) ©karamysh/Shutterstock.com, (b) ©connel/Shutterstock.com. **110** (t) ©Robert Harding Picture Library Ltd/Alamy, (b) ©Martin Thomas Photography/Alamy. **112** (t) ©Kichigin/Shutterstock.com, (b) ©Viacheslav Lopatin/Shutterstock.com. **114** ©craftvision/Getty Images, (b) ©Kreangkrai Indarodom/Shutterstock.com. **122** ©Jupiterimages/Brand X Pictures/Getty Images. **124** (t) ©Diego Cervo/Shutterstock.com, (b) ©sosogulz/Shutterstock.com. **126** (t) ©Goodluz/Shutterstock.com, (b) ©Cultura/Alamy. **128** (t) ©Katherine Welles/Shutterstock.com, (b) ©auremar/Shutterstock.com. **130** (t) ©Orange Line Media/Shutterstock.com, (b) ©William Perugini/Shutterstock.com. **132** (t) ©mattomedia Werbeagentur/Shutterstock.com, (b) ©Tyler Olson/Shutterstock.com. **134** (t) ©Alan Bailey/Shutterstock.com, (b) ©Junial Enterprises/Shutterstock.com. **142** ©AVAVA/Shutterstock.com. **144** (t) ©D. Sharon Pruitt Pink Sherbet Photography/Getty Images, (b) ©Yukmin/Getty Images. **146** (t) ©Darren Baker/Shutterstock.com, (b) ©PeoplePix/Alamy. **148** (t) ©Paisan Changhirun/Shutterstock.com, (b) ©CEFutcher/Getty Images. **150** (t) ©Magicinfoto/Shutterstock.com, (b) ©Roxana Gonzalez/Shutterstock.com. **152** (t) ©Getty Images, (b) ©Fer Gregory/Shutterstock.com. **154** (t) ©Getty Images, (b) ©Marmaduke St. John/Alamy.